THE ELIMINATION OF CHILD LABOUR: WHOSE RESPONSIBILITY?

The Elimination of Child Labour: Whose Responsibility?

A Practical Workbook

Pramila H. Bhargava

SAGE PUBLICATIONS
New Delhi ✦ Thousand Oaks ✦ London

DEC 03 2003

Copyright © Pramila H. Bhargava, 2003

First published in 2003 by

Sage Publications India Pvt Ltd
B-42, Panchsheel Enclave
New Delhi 110 017

Sage Publications Inc
2455 Teller Road
Thousand Oaks, California 91320

Sage Publications Ltd
6 Bonhill Street
London EC2A 4PU

Published by Tejeshwar Singh for Sage Publications India Pvt Ltd, typeset by Star Compugraphics Private Limited, New Delhi in 10/12 Baskerville and printed at Chaman Enterprises, Delhi.

Library of Congress Cataloging-in-Publication Data

Bhargava, Pramila H., 1966–
   The elimination of child labour: whose responsibility?: a practical workbook/
Pramila H. Bhargava.
   p. cm.
   Includes bibliographical references.
   1. Child labor–India. I. Title
HD6250.I42 B47   331.3'1'0954–dc21   2002   2002026889

ISBN: 0–7619–9616–8 (US–Hb)   81–7829–200–9 (India–Hb)
     0–7619–9617–6 (US–Pb)   81–7829–201–7(India–Pb)

Sage Production Team: Shweta Vachani, Rajib Chatterjee and Santosh Rawat

To
My mother, Rita Hingorani,
who taught me the value of education.

CONTENTS

LIST OF TABLES AND FIGURES

LIST OF ABBREVIATIONS

APC/DPEP	:	Additional Project Coordinator/DPEP
ASWO	:	Assistant Social Welfare Officer
BC	:	Backward Caste
CPO	:	Chief Planning Officer
DCF	:	Deputy Conservator of Forest
DD/SW	:	Deputy Director/Social Welfare
DE	:	District Engineer
DEO	:	District Education Officer
DM/Housing	:	District Manager for Housing Department
DPEP	:	District Primary Education Programme
DTWO	:	District Tribal Welfare Officer
DWCRA	:	Development of Women & Child in Rural Areas
FPP	:	Family Planning Programme
GCDO	:	Girl Child Development Officer
JVV	:	Jana Vignana Vedika, a youth group
MMS	:	Mandal Mahila Samakhya
MRO	:	Mandal Revenue Officer
MRP	:	Mandal Resource Person
MV	:	Mamidipudi Venkatarangaiah Foundation (an NGO)
NGO	:	Non-governmental Organisation
PD/DRDA	:	Project Director/District Rural Development Agency
PROBE	:	Public Report on Basic Education
RUDSET	:	Rural Development and Self Employment Training Institute (17 centres in India)
SAPAP	:	South Asian Poverty Alleviation Programme
SC	:	Scheduled Caste
ST	:	Scheduled Tribe
SW	:	Social Welfare
UNDP	:	United Nations Development Programme
VAO	:	Village Administrative Officer
VDO	:	Village Development Officer
VO	:	Village Organisation
YIP	:	Young India Project (an NGO at Anantapur)

FOREWORD

It is unfortunate that even today the problem of child labour is prevalent to a great extent in our country and in the world. The latest statistics show that about 250 million child workers exist in the age group of 5–14 all over the world. A recent survey conducted by the International Labour Organisation (ILO) states that out of these 61 per cent are in Asia, 32 per cent in Africa and 7 per cent in Latin America. India has the largest number of child labourers. It is also true that child labour in India is more of a rural phenomenon with more than 90 per cent children working in agricultural and allied activities in the villages. Children are important assets of any nation as they are the future citizens. The destiny of a country depends directly on how well its children are looked after.

Though clear provisions have been made in our Constitution to safeguard the interests of children by ensuring that they receive education and are not forced to work for a living, factors such as neglect of disadvantaged regions/communities, shortage of resources and the misconception that child labour supplements the family income have led to the continuance of child labour and the failure of the programme on compulsory primary education.

In June 2000, I visited the child labour residential camp at Peddavaduguru village in the Anantapur district of Andhra Pradesh, run by Ms Pramila H. Bhargava, a civil servant of the 1988 batch who was working on deputation as Consultant on primary education and child labour elimination for the National Poverty Alleviation Project. The progress achieved by all child labour girls in this camp was heart warming. The atmosphere was most conducive to the all round development of the girls.

Ms Pramila H. Bhargava has compiled her field notes and experiences and has authored this book which gives an honest picture of the child labour problem. It narrates the work done in an area which is drought prone, dominated by extremists, very backward and where incidence of rural child labour is very high. The book, along with the model workbook, effectively narrates how the government, community and NGOs can work together for the eradication of this social evil.

The book focuses on the need for the convergence of various departments and ministries as a pre-requisite for the elimination of child labour. A project can be run successfully only if various government departments involved are brought together, which would not only serve to minimise the total expenditure but also yield the desired result.

One strength of the book is that the author has supplemented it with a workbook, which describes the processes adopted by her. It can serve as a guide/manual for people who want to work in this field.

The elimination of child labour is not an impossible task. All that is required is appropriate action in the right direction. The author has correctly pointed out that over the years this responsibility has gradually shifted to the NGOs and private social organisations. No NGO is sufficiently equipped to handle this widespread socioeconomic problem, but if reputed NGOs are supported by all departments of the government, it can lead to success.

I commend the book to all those interested in the elimination of child labour. The merit of the book is that it is both analytical and practical.

4 July 2002   C. Rangarajan
                                             Governor of Andhra Pradesh
                                                                Hyderabad

PREFACE

Nothing in this world can take the place of persistence. Talent will not: Nothing is more common than unsuccessful people with talent, Genius will not: Unrewarded genius is almost a proverb, Education will not: the world is full of educated derelicts. Persistence and determination alone are omnipotent. The slogan 'press on' has solved and always will solve the problems of the human race.

—Calvin Coolidge

The above quotation closely echoed my feelings as I sat down to record an attempt to eliminate child labour in the Anantapur district of Andhra Pradesh (AP). The project had been beset by hardships forcing me to often contemplate giving up. However, something kept me going and propelled me to find a meaningful resolution to the problem. This book is an account of my battle against the menace of child labour. Fortunately, success did come in many ways.

Mr K. Raju, National Project Co-ordinator, UNDP, once suggested to me that I should write a book about my experiences, an idea that I did not entertain seriously at that time. However, certain events motivated me to write the book. After the end of my tenure as National Consultant I returned to Hyderabad, and soon after my arrival in the city, I fractured both my ankles in an accident and had to be confined to bed for a period of two months. During that time, villagers, teachers, members of women's groups, wardens of government hostels, officials and even local politicians travelled from Anantapur district to visit me. There were also an incredible number of letters from the rehabilitated children in the residential camps, all wishing me a speedy recovery. I felt deeply touched and gratified by the support and affection that I received. At that time, I chanced to read Coolidge's inspiring words on the power of persistence quoted in a newspaper and they kept haunting me. It then occurred to me that I was perhaps being granted time off from active work for a definite purpose.

I entered the ranks of bureaucracy after passing the civil services examination and was assigned work in the Indian Railway Personnel Service (IRPS) in 1989. During the next 13 years of my career, I served in various capacities and worked to gain valuable experience in administrative matters as well as in personnel management and labour welfare activities.

Even though my work was fulfilling, I was persistently haunted by a powerful yearning to tread new ground and achieve something other than what was simply routine or ordinary. As if it were an answer to my restlessness, I was deputed to work with the UNDP on 12 February 1999. At that time, UNDP was running a national programme on poverty alleviation in three districts of Andhra Pradesh and I was appointed as the national consultant for primary education and child labour elimination.

The percentage of child labour found in Andhra Pradesh is 14.3 per cent, which is the highest in India, and 90 per cent of child labour is employed in the rural areas. Anantapur, where I worked, is one of the largest districts in Andhra Pradesh, a region plagued with frequent droughts and the related evils of unemployment, poverty, illiteracy and child labour. Thus, the task was undoubtedly a challenging one. Also, my interest to continuously learn and explore different areas made the assignment an exciting as well as a fulfilling one.

Mr K. Raju suggested that I survey the situation personally and so, I visited work sites to observe children employed as labourers in quarries, groundnut, cotton fields and those engaged in cattle grazing and silk weaving. I also studied the situation in 36 schools in the district in order to understand the percentage causes of dropout cases among the village children. The results were disturbing, for it came to light that the first 20 villages had 903 child labourers. I immediately drew up a plan for community mobilisation and subsequently initiated the process of rescuing the children from their workplaces. I hoped to streamline these children towards education by using government programmes and designing others suited for the purpose.

Never once at the time of taking on the project did I comprehend the enormity of the problem of child labour. It was only as work progressed that I came to realise how widely extant the social evil was and how far-reaching its effects were. I found myself battling against innumerable and insurmountable odds such as paucity of funds, lack of support staff, mental tension and physical stress. Surrounded by a deluge of problems, I feared the programme would collapse and felt dejected and helpless.

The questions that most often haunted me during the time I was depressed were—how could a small effort change the situation and could I really make a difference? It was at that juncture that Sri Satya Sai Baba consoled and motivated me with his words of encouragement. I learnt to recognise and respect the powerful role of motivation in getting things done.

Finally, when I left at the end of the contract, a functional model was established that was cost-effective and hence viable. Some of the breakthrough I was able to achieve were: convergence of various government departments in solving the problem of child labour, the setting up of residential camps for the child labourers, involvement of the community and the introduction of vocational skills along with formal training.

I got completely absorbed in the work only to derive an immense sense of personal triumph and satisfaction. I had finally succeeded in streamlining the lives of 2,120 child labourers and even today 300 grown-up child labourers in residential camps are assured of a decent elementary education along with food and other necessities.

The Anantapur programme brought into light the vicious circle of poverty, illiteracy, child labour and unemployment. A large section of child labourers in our country belong to the backward castes that include Scheduled Castes, Scheduled Tribes and Other Backward Castes, and the key to their upliftment is literacy which alone can infuse a feeling of self-esteem and confidence in them. In fact, it has been established beyond doubt that there is a direct link between illiteracy and backwardness with 10 least literate districts of the country also being the most backward (*The Hindu*, 22 January 2001). It is thus vital to first deal with illiteracy as the major cause for backwardness. This should be done along with a simultaneous effort to make labour laws stringent otherwise India even after 55 years of independence will remain as one of the most backward nations.

This task cannot be seen as the responsibility of NGOs alone. We have successfully demonstrated how the state governments can also play a crucial role by making use of various government schemes as well as different departments and ministries. Furthermore, in the case of the Anantapur project, not a single volunteer had to be appointed. The services of MRPs who are teachers in local government schools more than sufficed in the accomplishment of our objective while also saving us a great deal of expenditure.

Developing countries of Asia that include India, Pakistan, Bangladesh and Sri Lanka spend absurdly huge amounts on defence. One wonders why we cannot simply forget our differences and instead use the available resources for the upliftment and ultimate elimination of child labour. This would make us a nation rich in human resources.

The book is not just a narration of the hardships likely to be encountered by one working in the field but also an account of valuable experiences that could guide anyone interested in this area of work. The book is not meant to be a mere portrayal of the pathetic condition and agony of millions of wretched child labourers in our country. On the contrary, it offers a definite model that has been evolved to successfully deal with the problem and includes a practical workbook at the end containing the course of action to be taken. I have always believed in finding a practical solution to any problem and this is the essence of my book.

Being neither a professional writer nor an expert in the writing field, I perceive my work as only a small but sincere attempt to tackle the problem of child labour and harbour the strong hope that the proposed model may indeed contain the germ of what could very well be the final solution itself. With due respect to the many experts working in the area, I believe that my practical work speaks with conviction about the crucial role that the government can play in the eradication of illiteracy and child labour with active support drawn from the community itself. Speaking at the National Conference of Child labour Organised by the labour ministry, Prime Minister A.B. Vajpayee stressed the need for such a joint effort to root out the problem and specially pointed to the significant role of district collectors in this regard (*The Hindu*, 23 January 2001).

PM for joint efforts to tackle child labour

If district collectors develop the will to write a success story in this regard, the task would become simpler. They ought to do everything from inspiring people to strictly enforcing the law against child labour.

My programme was also designed and implemented under the chairmanship of the District Collector. Engaging at such close quarters with poverty and the dismal plight of the child labourers of Anantapur made me work like one possessed until I was all-in-one, i.e., National Consultant cum Project Manager cum Community Coordinator and Community Volunteer.

There have been dark moments of bitterness and anger too, especially at being misunderstood or in having to literally ask for small things such as blankets, clothes and various other items for the rescued children. But today, with a workable convergent model and three residential camps as the outcome of my labour, 68 children passing Class VII in a short span of one and a half years, and at the state level, four children in 2001 and nine in 2002 got admission in the Andhra Pradesh Residential School, I am convinced that the indescribable job satisfaction I have enjoyed is well worth all the pain endured. I have also learnt that while working on such noble projects, one has to forget the self and all sense of shame or humiliation in seeking assistance from all available resources.

The work carried out is a small drop in the vast ocean of this social evil, but I believe that it is a practical model that has been implemented, tested and can be replicated by the government.

Finally, I wish to assert that the credit for this work is undeniably not entirely mine, being as it is a clear reflection of the labour of a team of people who worked in close association with me. The work owes whatever success it may be attributed with to innumerable people—family, friends, women and youth groups, teachers, government officials and the villagers themselves. The sale proceeds of this book will go towards the education of orphan child labourers of Anantapur.

Pramila H. Bhargava, IRPS
e-mail: pramila9000@yahoo.co.in

ACKNOWLEDGEMENTS

I express my sincere and heartfelt thanks to Sri Satya Sai Baba, whose motivation helped me in the 'Elimination of child labour' project. He also helped in the reconstruction of old buildings and providing stationery and watches for the children in the residential camps. I am indebted to Mr K. Raju (IAS), National Project Coordinator of the United Nations Development Project who gave me unstinted support and exemplary guidance in achieving my cherished goal, and also to all project personnel working under him.

My sincere thanks to Mr Anantha Venkata Rami Reddy (ex-Member of Parliament), Mr Parthasarathy, Mr Saifulla and Mr K. Srinivasulu, Members of Parliament who donated funds from the Member of Parliament Local Area Development Scheme (MPLADS) for the Project. I extend my special thanks to the Members of Legislative Assembly representing Peddavaduguru and Hindupur constituencies for their support and encouragement. It is noteworthy to mention that Mr C.C. Venkata Ramudu, MLA from Hindupur, who provided the necessary infrastructure for the schools, has now shouldered the responsibility of the programme after my withdrawal.

My deep gratitude to all the district officials who unremittingly supported me in the process of convergence.

At the mandal and village level, I am thankful to the people who worked on the field—Mandal Education Officers, Mr Narasimha Murthy, Ms Nagalakshmi and Mr Hussainappa; Mandal Revenue Officers, Mr Govindarajulu, Mr Kondiah and Mr Ziaullah; Ms Venkatalakshmi, Mandal Parishad Development Officer; Mr Ranganayakulu, Revenue Inspector, Hindupur; and Mr Das, Office Superintendent, Peddavaduguru mandal for their valuable contribution. I am also thankful to Mandal Resource Persons (DPEP), Mr Sudhakar Babu, Mr Narayanaswamy, Mr Ramakrishna, Mr Javed, Mr Thippeswamy, Mr Vijay Bhaskar, Ms Shyamlamma, Mr Venkateswaralu and Ms Sridevi, who extended full support for the success of my endeavour. Assistant Social Welfare Officers, Mr Rama Das and Ms Saraswati and Wardens, Mr Samuel and Mr Sudhakar also deserve my thanks.

The Project became worthwhile as many people from different walks of life contributed to it. The Governor of Andhra Pradesh, Mr C. Rangarajan and the Governor of Karnataka, Ms Rama Devi contributed in significant amounts. My thanks to Mr Giri, Vice Chancellor of Sri Satya Sai University and Ms Y. Saraswati Rao, Vice Chancellor, Sri Krishna Devaraya University. To Father Ferrer and Ms Anne Ferrer, a Spanish couple who has established an NGO called Rural Development Trust, which provided clothes to the children. Many thanks also to Mr Hanumantha Reddy, a freedom fighter from Peddavaduguru district who provided clothing for the rehabilitated children. Special thanks to Mr K. Bham Suleman, my Project Secretary who provided secretarial assistance and was instrumental in bringing out my work in a suitable format, and to Mr T. Vijay Kumar who consistently guided and advised me during this period. And also, the Project Officer of the UNICEF, Ms Sudha Murali, who donated Rs 25,000 for the project, in memory of her mother Venkatamma, which will provide education to a few orphan child labourers. I am also grateful to the Jain Association who donated blankets, and to Mr Bhaskar Reddy who was thoughtful enough to gift the children tape recorders and educational cassettes.

I am also thankful to the Railways (my parent department), i.e., Mr Ramachandraiah (Steno at Guntakal), Mr K. Chakravarthy (Jr. Steno/ HQ) and Mr Venkatesh Prasad who rendered assistance for the documentation.

Thanks to Mr K.S. Sarma (IAS), CEO, Prasar Bharti and Mr Lakshmidhar Mishra, ex-Secretary of Labour for their inspiring letters, and to Mr P.L. Sanjeeva Reddy (IAS), Director, IIPA for his able guidance and for believing in my endeavour. Thanks also to M. Sambasiva Rao, IAS, NIRD, Dr R.R. Prasad, Mr Vidyasagar and Dr Suman Chandra.

Heartful thanks to all the villagers and the teaching community of Peddavaduguru and Hindupur for their unstinted support and co-operation. I am also grateful to the principals, teachers, staff, bridge course volunteers who have worked untiringly for this programme.

My work on this book would not have been possible without Devi who developed my thoughts with her powerful pen. My thanks to Alfee who inspired me with a particular style of writing and for her help in my work; to Shital for making the process of editing a genuinely stimulating one and for giving the book its final shape; and to my friends, Lalita, Ushananda, Amita, Pam, Sangeeta, Rekha Subba Reddy and Suvarna who stood by me. My immensely heartfelt thanks to my mother who made me realise the importance of education, to Shreya my daughter who not only put up with my anxieties and despair many times but also comprised on our time together; to my sisters, Sunita and Meenu for pushing me to write and Rajat Bhargava (IAS), my husband, without whose active involvement neither could the project have been embarked upon nor this book completed.

In the end, my special thanks to Omita of Sage Publications for placing her faith in me, and to Shweta for her patience and for enabling a systematic presentation of this book.

CHAPTER 1

CHILD LABOUR: AN INSIGHT

The definition of child labour constitutes any act where children between the age of 5 and 14 years are directly or indirectly forced to work at home or outside it. As a consequence, children are not only deprived of their dignity but also their freedom to play, and their scope to develop physically, mentally and emotionally is lost. These children are also denied education, which is a fundamental right and should be available to them under any circumstances. It is unfortunate that even today the problem of child labour is greatly prevalent in our country and in the world. While, the latest statistics show that about 250 million child workers exist all over the world, a recent survey conducted by the International Labour Organisation (ILO) states that out of these, 61 per cent are in Asia, 32 per cent in Africa and 7 per cent in Latin America.

These child labourers are paid a meagre sum for all their hardships, which generally fails to ensure even one square meal a day. Driven to work at a crucial formative age and burdened with hard labour these ill-fated children are deprived of nutritious food, playtime and education. They lead miserable lives, devoid of simple childhood pleasures and do not even get the opportunity to develop into valuable human resource.

Children are important assets of any nation, they are the future citizens. The destiny of a country depends directly on how its children are nurtured to fulfill the requirements of its society. In India, education is the joint responsibility of both the state and central governments, and the Constitution of India envisages free and compulsory education for all children till the age of 14. Ironically, in reality, large numbers are denied this fundamental right and are subjected to back-breaking labour in pathetic conditions. The result is illiteracy—a factor inseparably linked with child labour.

Child labour policy in India concentrates more on amelioration than on total abolition. Only 3.6 per cent of India's gross national product (GNP) is spent on education. Lack of political will, shortage of resources and the misconception that child labour supplements the family income are some of the primary factors that lead to the failure of compulsory primary education. Lack of educational facilities, inadequate supervision and neglect of disadvantaged regions/communities are also responsible for this dismal performance.

GLOBAL SCENARIO: SOUTH ASIAN COUNTRIES

As per international comparisons in the area of education, India fails to find a position. It possesses the dubious distinction of having the world's largest number of out-of-school children (22 per cent of the global total) and adult illiterates (30 per cent of the global total population). An average adult in India spends a little over two years in school compared to five years in China, seven years in Sri Lanka and nine years in South Korea. During the last 50 years, many countries have overtaken India in the field of elementary education, and the best example is China, which faced problems of mass illiteracy and poverty similar to India in the 1940s. Today, China is far ahead of India as far as elementary education is concerned. Sri Lanka has also succeeded in bringing down the percentage of child labour by strict imposition of compulsory education.

Only 40.8 per cent of Indians over the age of 15 are literate. India, in fact, has a lower literacy rate than a large number of African countries, many of which, in comparison, have lower per capita incomes. Many low income countries with higher levels of illiteracy spend equal or higher proportions of their GNP on education. To put it simply, India not only spends less on education but also whatever it spends is concentrated on higher education. Thus, to ensure the elimination of child labour, we need to universalise primary school education. I agree it is not that simple, therefore, I have tried to provide arguments and possible solutions in this book.

SOME ARGUMENTS

Clear provisions have been made in our Constitution to safeguard the interests of children by ensuring education instead of forcing them to work for a living.

There are numerous provisions such as Articles 23, 24, 39(e) and (f), 41, 45 and 47 in our Constitution which prohibit the employment of children and also ensure free education. In spite of the constitutional safeguards listed above, it is distressing that illiteracy and the concomitant evil of child labour are highly pronounced in our country. Primary education is the most effective way of keeping children from becoming part of the labour force. However, in India, neither is primary education made compulsory nor child labour considered illegal. In actual practice, it is an accepted fact. As a result, we have an incredibly large number of child labourers (13.6 million to 44 million) in our country. Child labour constitutes 5.2 per cent of the total labour force and is more of a rural phenomenon with more than 90 per cent children working in villages.

The schooling system within the nation also varies from one state to another. However, few states like Kerala have created impressive records in the field of compulsory education. Kerala has the distinction of attaining 100 per cent literacy among its population. There are also states such as Tamil Nadu and Himachal Pradesh that are producing good results in the field of universal education. How is it that some attempts towards ensuring total literacy have met with success in other developing countries as well as in a few states of our country, while it has not yielded results in most parts of India?

100 Per Cent Literacy in Kerala: A Success Story

Kerala spends more on education than any other state government. The commitment of both the government and the people has produced impressive educational statistics. An important feature of education in Kerala is that all children between the age-group of 6–11 years are in school and enrolment in the age-group of 11–14 years is about 90 per cent. Another impressive fact is that all the children enrolled in primary schools have completed their primary education.

Educational growth in Kerala can be traced not only to the planning efforts and commitment of the government but also to the participation of non-governmental organisations, missionaries and the endeavours of the ancient princely states. Missionary schools have given particular attention to the education of women and the lower castes. They have also laid emphasis on technical education. The Kerala government spends Rs 64 per capita on education compared to Rs 33 spent in other states. Therefore, Kerala has devoted its educational resources to mass education rather than higher education (universities). Anganwadis have been located in 99 per cent of the villages. Land reforms as well as minimum wage laws have also been implemented. The reasonably high minimum wage also contributes by allowing parents to manage without the support of their children.

The Government of Kerala has made no special efforts to end child labour. It is the expansion of the school system rather than the enforcement of labour legislation that has reduced the menace of child labour in the state.

LITERACY IN ANDHRA PRADESH

India is divided into 28 states and Andhra Pradesh is the fifth largest state in terms of area and population. It is divided into 23 districts which are further divided into 1,122 mandals, 26,613 villages and 67,505 habitations. The literacy rate here is 54 per cent. This figure is rather low when compared to the national average of 62 per cent. The literacy rate is 43 per cent for females and 64 per cent for males (Tables 1.1 and 1.2), which is low compared to the national rate of 50 per cent and 73 per cent for females and males respectively. A report in *Deccan Chronicle* (6 October 2000) says that:

> Though the literacy rate in other States has increased over the years, Andhra Pradesh has lagged behind in improving its position. The National Sample Survey 1997 had ranked AP 23rd among backward states at 54 per cent literacy due to higher dropouts. Presently, 1.85 crore people are estimated to be illiterate in the state. In the 1997 survey, AP had the dubious distinction of

Table 1.1

Gender-wise Literacy Rates in Four Southern States in the 1991 Census and the National Sample Survey, 53rd Report 1997

State	1991 Census				53rd Round Sample Survey			
	Male	Female	Total	Rank among States	Male	Female	Total	Rank among States
Andhra Pradesh	55.13	32.72	44.09	19	64	43	54	23
Karnataka	67.26	44.34	56.04	15	66	50	58	19
Kerala	93.62	86.17	89.81	1	96	90	93	2
Tamil Nadu	73.75	51.33	62.66	7	80	60	70	13
INDIA	64.13	39.29	52.21	–	73	50	62	–

Sources: 1) Census of India, 1991.
2) Statistical Abstract, 1998, C.S.O., New Delhi.

Table 1.2
The Gross Enrolment Ratios of Four Southern States during 1998–99

State	I–V			VI–VII		
	Boys	Girls	Total	Boys	Girls	Total
Andhra Pradesh	87.28	83.07	85.20	52.31	41.66	47.07
Karnataka	111.35	104.38	107.90	70.94	61.06	66.08
Kerala	88.69	87.00	87.86	97.15	93.24	95.22
Tamil Nadu	109.47	107.10	108.31	97.67	87.94	92.91
INDIA	100.86	82.85	92.14	65.27	49.08	57.58

Source: Selected Educational Statistics, 1998–99, Ministry of Human Resource Development.

being the last among the southern States. Kerala accounted for the highest literacy rate of 93 per cent followed by Tamil Nadu at 70 per cent, and Karnataka at 58 per cent.

Incidentally, Andhra Pradesh has the highest percentage of child labourers which is 14.3 per cent of the entire nation's child labour population. As per the data published by V.V. Giri National Labour Institute, the total number of child labourers in Andhra Pradesh is 1,661,940. This is because of inadequate infrastructure, extreme backwardness, and poverty which is responsible for many social evils. Thus, it is not uncommon to find newspaper reports on children being sold as slaves or instances of helpless children being driven to work.

CHILDREN WORKING IN RURAL AREAS OF ANDHRA PRADESH

AGRICULTURAL LABOURERS

Children working as agricultural labourers are engaged in fields where groundnut, chilli, cotton and sunflower are produced.

BONDED OR CONTRACT LABOURERS

Children who are bonded or contract labourers are assigned different kinds of tasks each day. They are not allowed to go home but are forced to work irrespective of the time of the day, and they often go without food or rest.

CATTLE GRAZERS

Children working as cattle grazers are given the task of cattle grazing either by the landlords or by the parents themselves.

DOMESTIC WORKERS

In their own homes, children are assigned the work of taking care of younger siblings and are also entrusted with varied household duties like cooking, cleaning, washing clothes, dishes and other such chores. When engaged in domestic work (in other houses), children are burdened with heavy work that takes up their entire day and they are not allowed to go home until it is finished.

COTTAGE INDUSTRY WORKERS

As a result of economic development, many lucrative cottage industries are flourishing in the rural areas. Village children are often engaged in large numbers in cottage industries such as silk weaving and carpet making. This forces them to stay in cramped and dark interiors for long hours.

QUARRY WORKERS

Rural children are often engaged in quarries, mines and construction sites which often prove dangerous to their healths.

MY ASSOCIATION WITH THE PROJECT

The South Asian Poverty Alleviation Programme (SAPAP) was an ambitious and challenging initiative taken up by United Nations Development

Programme (UNDP) in 1994 to support the SAARC countries. This was a national project designed to alleviate poverty. It was operating in six countries—Bangladesh, India, Maldives, Nepal, Pakistan and Sri Lanka.

In India, this national project was operating in three drought-prone districts of Andhra Pradesh—Mahabubnagar, Kurnool and Anantapur. The programme mainly concentrated on micro-credit, thrift and savings. In 20 mandals of these three districts, 2,458 self-help groups were formed from the population which was below the poverty line. Membership was given to the disadvantaged groups in the society.

The programme packages are largely focussed on economic activities and reduction of poverty, whilst the interest of the communities extend beyond this to embrace other dimensions of poverty including social concerns such as health and education. Large number of child labourers were found in these groups. Therefore, I was appointed as National Consultant on Primary Education and Child Labour Elimination.

Anantapur district (after Jaisalmer in Rajasthan), is known for its meagre rainfall and is a desert-prone area. This district regularly suffers from a series of droughts resulting in severe poverty. Villages are located at far distances from each others, and in case of no rainfall even seasonal work is not available to the villagers. These are some of the reasons why the District of Anantapur was selected for this project.

Anantapur is the largest district of Andhra Pradesh in terms of area. It comprises 63 mandals and is spread over 19,130 sq km. Out of the 3.18 million population, 2.47 million people are from villages. As per the V.V. Giri National Labour Institute's data, Anantapur has 92,255 child labourers. My work started with two mandals of Anantapur district— Peddavaduguru and Hindupur. One mandal usually consists of 40–60 villages.

Peddavaduguru mandal is situated on the southeastern side of Anantapur district and is a backward mandal. Hindupur is a semi-urban area. The town is a business centre for all the villages around it and is just 90 km away from the city of Bangalore, the capital of Karnataka. Both these mandals face a variety of problems, child labour being one of them.

For Anantapur district, which is the most backward and poorest district of Andhra Pradesh, nothing could be more important than education as a long-term investment in human resource development. However, as a district with a high rate of illiteracy and population scattered over a large geographical area, poor productivity of agricultural land, malnutrition, poverty and a very low premium on education, Anantapur demands greater conceptual clarity in planning and operationalising the package of measures to achieve primary education goals. Any long-term and sustainable programme would have to be multifaceted, involving a mix of a dynamic formal system together with flexible and innovative courses, active community participation and a host of creative methods to be evolved in consonance with the local cultural scenario.

CHAPTER 2

POVERTY AND SURVIVAL: OCCUPATIONS IN WHICH CHILDREN ARE ENGAGED

QUARRYING AND MINING

During my visit to Kristipadu village in Anantapur district, I visited the mines located between the Gooty mandal and Rayalacheruvu village of Yadiki mandal. As I came closer to a quarry, I noticed a group of young boys and girls carrying loads of crude minerals on their heads. The climate was hot and humid. The heat radiated by the stones was unbearable and I began to wonder how these children worked barefoot. I realised that these children were above the age-group of 6 braving the heat. When I approached the quarry owner, he was at first reluctant to answer any questions and asked the children to move away. After being assured that this was just a casual visit, he became more friendly. Hundreds of children

The son of today, the man of tomorrow protecting his head from the heat of life

Load of responsibility too heavy at this tender age

were busy working in the quarries, most of them from backward castes. They were doing night shifts also. Upon asking one of the children about the scorching heat emanating from the stones that would harm his feet, he replied that it was because he could be on the move all the time that he did work. He made sure that he did not stay at any place too long. Some children also expressed fear of the big stones rolling down and hurting them. Accidents of this kind were quite frequent.

Stone quarrying is a major industry in Anantapur district. It thrives and flourishes only due to child labour which is easily available. Huge amounts of limestone is also found in this district. L&T Cements and Pennar Cements are the two major industries in this area which use this limestone.

SOME FACTS

Quarries are of two kinds, small (*chinna gani*) and big (*pedda gani*). There are 144 such quarries in the district which are generally leased out to interested parties, and the average cost of leasing one hectare is about Rs 30,000 per annum, or Rs 80 per ton of stone, whichever is higher.

People from the backward caste community are employed on the construction sites and also in the mining fields.

VARIETIES OF STONE

Once the stone is mined and brought up to the surface, it is sorted into different varieties. After further processing and clarifying, the varieties can be classified as granite, dolomite, steatite, shale and clay.

GRANITE

The granite mined at Anantapur is pink in colour and is used extensively in the western countries for making pavements. Shaped into kerbs and tubes, the granite is loaded into trucks and transported to Chennai, from where it is shipped to distant parts of the world. In the USA, granite is sold at the rate of $45–$50 per ton. The waste material which is left over after granite is produced is grey in colour and is known as road metal. It is crushed in stone crusher and used for building concrete, concrete slabs and in laying roads.

**Stone is exported to countries like the
USA and is also used to make pavements**

DOLOMITE

Dolomite is mainly used by the steel industries as a purifying agent of
hematite, i.e., iron ore. Dolomite, which is extracted at the intermediary
stage in the district, is used by Zindal Steel Industries and Satavahana
Industries at Bellary. Another steel factory that is coming up near Tadipatri
will increase the demand further.

STEATITE

Steatite (soapstone) can be extracted only after attaining a depth of
70–75 feet. At Rayalacheruvu mandal, steatite is pulverised into fine
powder and exported to Chennai, Salem and other cities. Steatite is used
to make talcum powder, toothpowder and in the manufacture of certain
kinds of paint.

SHALE

It is black in colour and used for the manufacture of gemaxine.

CLAY

Known as 'white aluminium', clay is used in the manufacture of sanitary ware.

PATTERN OF WORK AND PAYMENT

Work starts early in the morning. In summer, it starts around 5 a.m. and ends by 11 a.m. In winter, the timings are between 7 a.m. and 1 p.m.

The grinding poverty of these people makes them vulnerable and easy to exploit by the greedy sub-contractors. Children are sincere and perform the assigned job without any protest. Their wages are low compared to those of the adults. As per my study, the average daily income of many such families is less than Rs 50. Most of them can barely afford a single meal per day. Under these circumstances, it is not surprising that young children work in the treacherous stone quarries. At the end of a day, a child earns something between Rs 15 and Rs 20 for enduring excruciating hardships. It is a common phenomenon in many parts of the country and most people do not consider it unnatural to employ children.

No parents would like their child to work in a quarry under such terrible conditions unless they are left with no choice. Due to their poor economic background, they are forced to send their children into the quarries in order to earn a livelihood.

After a lot of persuasion, Ediletiamma, a woman worker in the quarry agreed to talk about her experiences and what she thought about the education of child labourers. Ediletiamma lives in Harijanawada area of Kristipadu village situated in the Peddavaduguru mandal. She says,

> I have sent my son to school. I know it will be good if he pursues education. I also advise my neighbours to do the same. However, they often question me about what one gains from being educated. They have lost faith in the system ... do you know we have one school but it has only one room. What kind of a school is that? I also sometimes agree with my neighbours. I feel there is no solution for us as this is a drought stricken backward area. Therefore, most of us are forced to make our children work. How will we survive otherwise? Do you think we are not aware of the hardships our children face ... which parent would not want his child to go to school? I guess we have to just reconcile with our fate.

Ediletiamma also pointed out that though the government provides free education, parents also have to spend some amount from their side. This fact has been confirmed by the report on education conducted by PROBE. According to several surveys that were conducted in many PROBE villages, the minimum amount that a family has to incur towards education is Rs 318 annually.

**Life breaking poverty forcing children
to work in stone breaking quarry**

OCCUPATIONAL HAZARDS

A section of quarrying involves the crushing of stones to powder. In the powder factories there are several children and they are forced to breathe the powder that is permanently present in the air. Most children do not wear any masks. They are easily prone to various respiratory ailments, such as silicosis, asthma and tuberculosis, apart from other forms of illnesses.

Mining is taken up in phases and at a particular stage, it has to be done through blasting. Generally blasting is done after normal working hours when the labourers have left. However, sometimes a couple of detonators are left behind in an unexploded condition. These have led to several accidents especially when barefooted children have unknowingly stepped on these unexploded detonators. In spite of all these hazards, the children are sincere and do their work without any protest.

Bhaskar Reddy, a labourer, commenting on the accidents and hazards said, 'It is quite common for us to receive injuries. We don't perceive it as a hazard. We are now habituated to this kind of work and learn to adjust at the earliest.'

Conclusion: A Working Solution

While poverty is the main reason behind the abuse of child labour in this particular area, there are other factors also which contribute to this. One such is the lack of proper schools. In the Harijanawada area in the Kristipadu village, there was just a one-room school where all children, irrespective of age or class, had to sit together, tightly packed.

This problem was soon solved. One SC Corporation shed was discovered which had been lying unused for the past 10 years. With the help of the SC Corporation, the shed was repaired and four classrooms and an anganwadi was set up. We persuaded and convinced the parents to send their children to the new school. Around 70 children who were until then child labourers joined the school. However, not all children could join as they were the main breadwinners of their families. Then, evening classes were started and soon many grown-up child labourers joined eagerly. Therefore, one can conclude that the dual evils of poverty and lack of infrastructure directly create the problem of child labour.

Cotton Cultivation

Introduction

Andhra Pradesh is known for its cotton cultivation, given the fact that it has several areas with fertile black soil, which is ideal for the cultivation of this major cash crop. Peddavaduguru mandal is very famous for its cotton fields. As cotton requires less irrigation, most of the area under cultivation is devoted to cotton. Villages such as Appecherla, Virupapuram, Malenipalli and Peddavaduguru thrive entirely on cotton cultivation. It is common knowledge that in these areas, cotton growing is intensively cultivated, but what is not known is the prevalence of child labour.

USE AND ABUSE OF CHILD LABOUR

Child labour is utilised extensively for the cultivation of cotton. Why is this is so?

1. Surprising as it may seem, one prefers children to work in the cotton fields. Adults are not wanted here, and even in those rare cases when they are hired, they are paid much less. This is one area of rural labour where children get preference and are also paid more than adults. Children are paid Rs 20 per day, whereas adults get only Rs 10 per day.
2. A progressive farmer of this area, Sankar Reddy, asserts that many factors contribute towards the suitability of children for this type of work. Prime among them is the height factor. Since cotton bushes are short, the short height of children makes them ideal for work in cotton fields. Other factors are their general amenability to work, their fear of authority figures, as well as their comparatively docile nature. Together, all these factors contribute towards the overall use of child labour in these fields.
3. Landlords and businessmen from coastal Andhra take enormous tracts of land on lease for growing cotton. They then employ hundreds of children at very nominal sums to work in these fields. The children take care of agricultural operations and maintain the crops, while the landlords return to the cities. These young children toil under the sun, among pesticide covered crops and earn handsome profits for their contractors.

It is the middlemen or contractors who make a living from this entire business. They pay small amounts to the parents of these children and get many times more, for providing their services, from the field owners.

Cotton cropping can be classified into two types: commercial cropping and seed production. Pea-sized seeds are sown, one foot apart. In seven days time the seeds start sprouting and need irrigation. The high level canal (HLC-North) provides water to the eight villages, i.e., Peddavaduguru, Chinnavaduguru, Miduthuru, Dimmagudi, Chitturu, Kotarpalli, Medamakulapalli and Kandlaguduru. When the cotton plants reach the budding stage, a process called Hybridisation is implemented.

Far from schools, stuck in the fields

HYBRIDISATION OF COTTON

A small boy and girl doing hybridisation

Given this scenario, the main interest in growing cotton is for the purpose of seed production. This is because seed production fetches a higher price and is, therefore, definitely more profitable. The seed crop is ready in only about 180 days. Since less time is required and more income assured, this type of production is generally preferred here.

About 45 days after the sowing, buds start emerging. Generally, in the commercial crop, pollination occurs after this stage with the male and female flowers (androecium and gynaecium) coming together. However, this natural event has to be manually done in the case of seed variety cropping. First, the children physically remove the bud from the plant; this process is called 'emasculation'. After this cross-pollination has to be manually done by the children, whose size assists them in moving around easily among the cotton bushes. After this hybridisation process is over, each head is covered with cellophane paper and a red paper tag attached, which indicates that the plant has been hybridised.

The Economics of Cotton Cultivation

An agriculturist has to invest an approximate amount of Rs 1 lakh per acre. This includes the cost of seeds, fertilisers, pesticides, labour charges and all other agricultural operations. When harvest time approaches, the growers have to get the crop tested for genetic purity. This test is carried out by government agencies. Only when the crop is certified to having 99 per cent purity is it considered fit for harvesting. Otherwise the whole crop is rejected. Thus, the risk factor is very high, especially for the small and marginal farmers who have borrowed enormous amounts from moneylenders for the whole operation. When the crop fails, entire families are wiped out due to abject poverty, and as a result often many farmers commit suicide.

In the Killing Cotton Fields

I did a tour of several villages—Virupapuram, Mallenipalli, Lakshumpalli and Appecherla—in order to ascertain the main reasons for the prevalence of child labour in the areas under cotton cultivation. The reasons have already been mentioned above. I will not reiterate these facts here. But some other facts caught my attention, such as the health hazards faced by thousands of children who work in the pesticide drenched cotton fields. Young children, mainly girls, stand amidst the plants, bend over each to identify the flowers ready for pollination, and rub a male flower on to the identified female flower. Kalpana Sharma points out:

In the course of doing this work for many hours in the day, the children are exposed to pesticides like endosulpan, which is an organochlorine. The exposure affects the nervous system and symptoms of poisoning are precisely what these children have reported—headaches, weakness, disorientation, convulsions, and respiratory depression. This pesticide is used to combat American bollworm caterpillars, which penetrate the cotton flower buds. Also, organochlorines remain in the body for a long time (*The Hindu*, 24 December 2000).

This shocking situation is not common knowledge and rarely does the general public get to know about how traumatic the conditions are. However, for the farmers of this region and their families, this is an inescapable and unavoidable fact of their poverty stricken and debt-ridden lives.

Another fact that caught my attention was the method used by the labour contractors to control and discipline the poor children. Threats and coercive tactics are all too familiarly used. Very often corporal punishment is also used to instill fear. I recall one instance when I was visiting Appecherla village during the early days of the project, a contractor was trying to hide the children under the apprehension that they would be forcibly taken away to school. However, as I was a familiar figure to the children, they crowded around me. This did not stop the contractor's wife from using a stick to control them (as seen in the photograph here).

Landlady with stick, children are struck

I was fortunate to meet the Anantapur Rythu (farmers) President, Veera Reddy, who shared some thoughts on child labour with us. According to him,

> Most of us want children to study but when we see them wasting time and not attending school, I feel it is better to employ them. I do agree that children are more useful in the area of cotton cultivation due to their size and nature. Not only do they work fast, they are also obedient. However, if proper schooling facilities are made available I think even their parents will not mind enrolling them. Many adults in these villages are idle. We could always hire them. I personally have no objection in doing so. I also admit that contractors are selfish in employing children.

Rich landlords lure the poor farmers with money for their children's services. Anything between Rs 300 and Rs 400 is offered per month. This appears to be a princely sum for these abjectly downtrodden people. Work in the cotton fields is seasonal, so they grab whatever money is offered to them. But once the season is over they return to the grinding poverty of their lives. Peddavaduguru mandal is a drought-prone area, which breeds poverty and all its accompanying evils such as illiteracy, child labour, hunger, disease and death.

As Kalpana Sharma pointed out in her booklet on 'Memories of Drought in Andhra Pradesh',

> Andhra Pradesh, which has a geographical area of 2.75 lakh sq. km., has several districts, which are chronically drought prone. In particular, the districts in the Telengana [sic] region and in Rayalaseema encounter drought almost every alternate year because of inadequate rains.
>
> The average annual rainfall fell from 778 mm to only 534 mm in 1999. In 2000, 18 districts out of 23 districts were declared drought affected.[1]

The employment of children provides at least seasonal relief and so the people see it as a necessary evil. The sight of scores of children working hard under the hot sun, surrounded by pesticide dust in the cotton fields is very common in the Andhra Pradesh.

---

1. Sharma, Kalpana, 2000, 'Memories of Drought in Andhra Pradesh'. Hyderabad: UNICEF.

GROUNDNUT CULTIVATION

SOME FACTS

Anantapur district has minimum irrigation facilities, and compound to this pathetic condition, the rainfall in this geographical area is also scanty. Given this pattern of poor rainfall, the agriculturists in the area depend mostly on those crops which require minimum water. One such crop is groundnut.

A well known fact is that Anantapur district is a chronically drought-prone area and quite often the rainfall is meagre and scarce. When the monsoon season fails or when rainfall is severely inadequate, the groundnut crop fails completely leaving the farmers worse off than before.

Groundnut is grown in these areas as a monocrop and is cultivated by 90 per cent of the farmers in Anantapur. For sowing purposes, 50 kg of seed is used per acre. At the time when this study was carried out, each kg of seed was priced at Rs 20.

Eight days after sowing, the seeds start sprouting, an event which is much awaited by the farmers. After growing for about 120 to 130 days, the crop is ready for harvest as the nuts are well developed in the pods.

Working in the groundnut fields is a backbreaking job. Bending over or crouching under the groundnut bushes to weed or irrigate for long hours is both tiresome and monotonous. Children who should be allowed to play and have fun endure such labour for several hours at a stretch. This stunts their growth and overall development.

Groundnut harvesting is done by hand and six persons are required per acre for this activity. Per acre, 4 to 5 quintals of pods are produced. A quintal was priced at approximately Rs 1,250 at the time of this study. Generally, the standard term of measurement is one sack containing 42 kg of groundnuts, sold at a price of Rs 500.

Several allied industries surround the groundnut fields in Anantapur district. Kalluru is a village located near Peddavaduguru mandal and has a number of oil extraction mills. The remnants from the oil extraction are processed into cattle feed. These industries also make use of child labour.

Crop failure, either due to drought or due to pest attacks has become very common in Anantapur district. This district of Andhra Pradesh is the second most drought-affected district in the entire country after Jais-almer in Rajasthan. When the crops fail, the farmers whose lives depend on the harvest become absolutely hopeless and their poverty is beyond imagination. In the year of 1999, the cotton farmers of the Telangana region resorted to suicide due to bollworm attacks on their crop. In 2000, the groundnut farmers of Anantapur district faced a similar fate when the *Bud Necrosis* virus attacked the groundnut crop and many farmers committed suicide.

Approximately 1 million acres of the groundnut crop have fallen prey to this virus in Anantapur and Kurnool districts. Mohammed Saddiq, who writes for *The Economic Times* (6 October 2000) reported,

AP Ryots Embrace Death as Crops Fail

For the third time in two years, farmers in Andhra Pradesh are resorting to suicides after their crops had failed. At least 15 farmers have attempted suicide in the past month. Eight farmers have died, while seven others have been saved by timely medical intervention. Three girls also committed suicide, as they did not want to be a burden on their worried fathers. All of them were expecting to be married this year if the crop had not failed.

This time around, it is the groundnut crop that has been hit by the Bud Necrosis virus. Some one million acres of the groundnut crop in Anantapur and Kurnool districts have been affected. The crop in neighbouring Chittoor and Prakasam districts has also been hit. In Anantapur district alone, farmers fear they could lose Rs 1,500 crore worth of crop due to the virus attack.

Though the pesticide has proved ineffective against the virus, it has proved deadly for the farmers who have consumed it in a fit of desperation and frustration. Most of the victims are small farmers, for whom the destruction of the crop in 2000 came as the last straw.

Successive years of crop failure have broken the courage of even the most intrepid farmers, for instance, the case of Padmamma of Penakacherla as reported in *The Hindu* (20 September 2000). Padmamma was a widow with four children, who consumed pesticide as her groundnut crop in 3.5 acres was a failure. She died while undergoing treatment at the Anantapur General Hospital.

CHILD LABOUR AND GROUNDNUT CULTIVATION

Unlike in the other industries where children are used for specific reasons, in the groundnut fields they are used because there are never enough adults to do all the required work.

At the time of the harvest, labourers are required in large numbers at a short notice. During this critical period there is a very high demand for labour from all the different agriculturists, and adults being insufficient in number, children are pressed into service. Post harvest, 80 per cent of the children are employed in bundling the plants, arranging them into heaps and transporting them to the threshing ground. They also separate the nuts from the plants.

Child labourers participate enthusiastically in this work and are paid Rs 25 per day. This may seem like a very attractive sum, but one must remember that the harvest season is a very brief one and is over too soon. And when sometimes the groundnut crop fails totally due to the lack of rain, there is massive poverty and survival itself is at stake.

CATTLE GRAZING

We have seen how young children are thoroughly exploited both financially and physically. They never get the benefits of their hard work. In the process, they lose their childhood and their time for play. In short, they no longer remain children, instead they are forced to turn into miniature sized adults with all the responsibilities of breadwinners. We are depriving the entire nation of tomorrow when we abuse the young children of today.

Until now we have looked at the presence of child labour in the areas of cotton cultivation, mining and quarrying. In this section we shall take a closer look at the involvement of child labour in the area of cattle grazing.

BACKGROUND

The Hindupur area of Anantapur district is famous for its 'milk' and 'silk'. Situated near Karnataka, Hindupur mandal has been rearing crossbreed cows for several decades, and many of the key village schemes are related to this significant area of agrarian growth. All aspects of livestock development such as breeding, feeding and health care are taken care of along with the marketing aspects of cattle farming. Milk production is very high here despite the area being classified as 'drought prone'. According to the manager of the milk plant at Hindupur, 'The livestock industry is flourishing and the production of milk is so abundant that we have a surplus very often.' This surprised me as I had only been aware of the acute water scarcity in this area.

Some Facts about Livestock Production and Maintenance

As per the 1993 Census, Anantapur district has the following livestock population:

Table 2.1
Livestock Population in Anantapur District, 1993

White Cattle	6.30 lakh
Black Cattle	2.65 lakh
Sheep	8.79 lakh
Goats	2.75 lakh
Pigs	0.22 lakh
Poultry	9.33 lakh

At present the livestock population in Anantapur district is 22 lakh approximately.

Milch cows are present in large numbers and good care is taken of them because their milk fetches good money. Apart from the milch cows, there are a lot of drought bullocks which are maintained on the hay from the groundnut, jowar, redgram and horsegram harvests. Other cattle as well as the young stock is left to graze. The sheep in this district are reared essentially for their meat. Even though they are not reared for their wool, their hide is sold to local cobblers. Fodder is not a problem in this area as paddy, straw and groundnut husk is used to feed the cattle. The goats and sheep are also taken for open grazing.

Child Labour and Livestock Management

Upon enquiring from a local dairy manager about the involvement of children in the various activities relating to livestock management, he gave me all the relevant details regarding child labour in this industry. Children, mainly young boys, are hired on annual, biannual or multiple-year basis. A lumpsum amount is paid for their services. Generally, an

A child taking buffaloes for grazing

amount ranging between Rs 3,000 and Rs 4,000 is paid to every child annually for tending goats/sheep. This works out to be anything between Rs 8 to Rs 11 per day. For managing large animals they are paid between Rs 5,000 and Rs 6,000 per annum.

A major part of their day from 8 a.m. to 6 p.m. is spent out in the open, grazing the animals under their charge. Each child has to manage a flock of about minimum 50 animals. The children have to provide water to the flock, bring hay from the haystacks outside the village and also clean the sheds. In the case of large ruminants which are milked twice a day, the children have to prepare them for milking.

Certain diseases, such as Black Quarter (*Jabba Vapu*) haemorrhagic septicemia, liver fluke and worm infestations attack sheep. Some of them bleed to death if not treated on time. Liver fluke is a major cause of sheep mortality. The young shepherds have to be aware of these problems as

Food carried in a simple cloth and tied with nylon ropes

Yellappa along with two young shepherds enjoying lunch

well and report it to the owners. Apart from their regular duties many of them also have to help in the household chores. They sleep with their goats and sheep at night and have to be aware of what is generally going on.

Yellappa, a contract labourer shares his harsh life conditions with us and dimisses it as 'irony of fate':

> I am 13 years old. Every day I take the cattle out for grazing. After continuously working in the hot sun, I return late in the evening only to attend to more household work. In the night, I sleep with the cattle. I often carry a chikkem (food tied in a cloth with nylon ropes).

This food consists of cheap boiled rice with a little groundnut and chilli paste (called *pachadi* in this area). 'This is my feast when I am tired and hungry', says Yellappa.

When asked about his desire to be like the other children of his age-group—of whom some were studying—Yellappa frowned and remarked, 'I do not expect anything. It is the irony of my fate.' One does not really know if this is maturity, compelling adulthood or a compromise. Perhaps it is the irony of our system where child labour has become an accepted fact.

CONCLUSION

The use of child labour in livestock management is several centuries old. The hardships children face are far more than anything they earn, but still these children go on because it is their only way of survival. In most cases it is also the only mode of survival for their parents also. So this evil continues.

SERICULTURE

Silkworm rearing and the production of silk is an important industry in Anantapur district. Silk weaving is a significant cottage industry in these areas and is practised in many villages of the Hindupur and Dharmavaram mandals. The products made in these places are well known all over India, and there is a great demand for them both in Indian and the foreign markets. Peddavaduguru is another mandal where silk weaving has taken root and is flourishing.

SOME FACTS ABOUT SERICULTURE

Sericulture is the main cash crop in the Hindupur area and many of the ryots (farmers) here are involved in either the cultivation of silk worms or silk weaving. Mulberry trees are also grown and its leaves are fed to the silkworms which thrive on it. Many families are involved in mulberry cultivation and silkworm rearing. Children work in mulberry cultivation by picking leaves and feeding it to the worms. They also pick ripe worms

A small girl picking cocoons from 'Chandrike'

and put on the 'chandrike' for the formation of cocoons. Further, the children are active participants in the harvest of cocoons and, subsequently, in the grading of good and bad cocoons.

SILK WEAVING: A STORY

During a tour of villages in Anantapur district, I happened to run into a family of weavers. Feeling very thirsty, while walking down the dusty lanes of a village, I stopped at a house for water. The residents of the house were polite and curious to see me. An old man came out and invited me inside. He said, 'Yella neeru kaaya teesukondi, yendana badi vochaaru' (You have come in the scorching sun, take the coconut water).

While sipping coconut water, I heard a peculiar sound from inside the house. Upon inquiring about it the old man took me into the interiors of the house where a child sat, deeply engrossed in the weaving of a silk sari on a hand-run loom. The deftness with which he wove as well as the beauty of the piece amazed me. At that point, I also noticed some of the children of the house actively engaged in the dying and silk reeling work. This provoked my curiosity about the role of children in the silk weaving business.

CHILD LABOUR IN THE SILK WEAVING INDUSTRY

Generally the silk weaving enterprises in these villages are on a small scale and located in the houses of individual owners. A loom is purchased and installed in a room and the necessary thread from Dharmavaram are bought at the wholesale market. *Vaarpu* or white thread, which is used for the warp or vertical line, is procured along with *sub puri* which is the thread used for the horizontal line in the weave. *Zari*, or the threads used for glitter (gold or silver coloured), are also bought from the Dharmavaram market. Colours are added to the threads according to the requirements and the design. This process is called Addakam. A certain kind of expertise is essential for doing this work. Children are usually preferred because once they are trained they follow instructions obediently.

After the threads are procured and coloured as per the requirement, the actual weaving begins. The thread is attached to the loom and weaving starts. Intermittently the *zari* threads are added as required. Design sheets

A boy working on a loom

are available at Dharmavaram, one sheet costs around Rs 100. On an average, it takes seven days to weave a silk sari on a handloom.

There are several stages in the weaving process, and during some of these stages children are employed. As mentioned earlier, they colour the thread and they reel the thread into bobbins, for which they are paid Rs 120 per kg. Many times it is teenage children who do the actual weaving of a sari and for this they are paid an average of Rs 400 per sari. Silk weaving is a traditional occupation and the children of a family are trained from a young age in the various skills required for this occupation. Comparatively, the children engaged in the silk weaving industry are better off than the children in the mining industry or those who work in the cotton fields. They are also much better paid because the wages here are reasonable.

SOME OCCUPATIONAL HAZARDS

Despite the several comparative advantages of working in the silk weaving industry, it is a fact that this area is also full of hazards. Reeling the thread on spools raises a certain amount of fine dust which these children breathe in, and become easily susceptible to respiratory diseases. The dyes used for colouring threads contain strong chemicals which react harmfully on the tender skin of children. Here, many of the young children also suffer from some form of chemical poisoning.

However, one problem goes beyond all this. This is a universal problem that affects these children who are always indoors throughout the day. They are deprived of sunlight and fresh air, above all, they are not sent to school or educated.

CONCLUSION

Child labour, whether it is under the hot sun of the quarries, in the pesticide laden cotton fields, in the groundnut fields, the grazing meadows or amidst the clattering looms, all imply one thing, that is the distress of children who are deprived of what is rightfully theirs. As per the Ministry of Labour:

> Poverty is basic reason which compels parents of a child, despite their unwilling-ness, to get it employed. The Survey Report of the Ministry of Labour ... had also so stated. Otherwise, no parents, specially no mother would like that a tender aged child should toil in a factory in a difficult condition, instead of it enjoying its childhood at home under the paternal gaze.[2]

---

2. Government of India, 1998, 'Policy and Progrmme for the Rehabilitation of Working Children and Manual for the Implementation of National Child Labour Projects.' New Delhi: Ministry of Labour.

CHAPTER 3

LIBERATION THROUGH
FREEDOM AND EDUCATION

SURVEY

Any action undertaken in the area of elimination of child labour must necessarily be preceded by a first hand survey of the situation. Hence, I began an extensive tour of three mandals—Peddavaduguru, Gandlapenta and Hindupur in the Anantapur district of Andhra Pradesh. The villages visited were Chinnavaduguru, Dimmagudi, Muppalagooty, G. Venkatampalli, Kandlaguduru, Miduthuru, Kristipadu, Chitrachedu, Chitturu, C. Ramarajupalli, Rampuram, Gopurajupalli, Virupapuram, G. Anantapur, Ravuludiki, Konapuram, Bheemunipalli, Mallenipalli, Lakshumpalli, Appecherla, Kondupalli and Peddavaduguru in the Peddavaduguru mandal; Katakam Varipalli, Kantampalli and Muddannagari Palli in Gandlapenta mandal; and Kotnoor, Gollapuram, Chalivendala, Meenakuntapalli, Gollapuram, Chalivendala, C. Cherlopalli, Subbireddipalli, Melapuram, Shanthinagar and K.W. Colony in the Hindupur mandal.

The task was by no means an easy one. I had to travel long distances in the hot sun to visit remote village schools and carefully scan the school records. MRPs (teachers in the DPEP scheme), Sudhakar and Narayanaswamy, who accompanied me during the survey, proved to be veritable pillars of strength. National Project Coordinator, UNDP under whom I was working, also encouraged me to first study the system and then accordingly plan future course of action. Initially, we were met with an implacable, uncooperative attitude and a battery of tough questions from officials of the school and village bodies. Refused to be affronted, I tried to explain the study undertaken in a simple and direct manner. This brought about a gradual change in attitude, which was previously marked by indifference or arrogance.

The school committee chairman of Kandlaguduru village of Kadavaduguru mandal, in particular, was extremely vociferous in expressing his woes about inadequate infrastructure of the school.

Having broken the ice and made some headway as far as access to the village records went, I systematically gathered data to find two major discrepancies. One, it was clear that the number of children on the school rolls rarely matched with the number of students actually present in school. Two, the actual number of children engaged as labourers at various work sites were far more than what the available statistics indicated. This finding fully justified my decision to start the project with a fresh survey instead of depending on the available figures. It was decided that we should conduct a survey of strength as well as the actual attendance in schools.

The sample data presented in Tables 3.1 to 3.3 reveal the situation in three villages of Peddavaduguru mandal. First, it was found that the dropout rate had an alarming increase in direct proportion to the classes starting from Class I to Class V. Thus, in comparison with figures for Class I, those for Class V showed a dramatic fall of about 50 per cent. Second, it was clear that the dropout rate of girls was high.

Table 3.1
Class-wise Distribution of Students in the School in Kandlaguduru Village

Standard	Boys	Girls	Total
I	20	25	45
II	20	21	41
III	17	11	28
IV	14	7	21
V	17	4	21

Data collected at the primary school in Kandlaguduru village bears testimony to the magnitude of problem of dropouts. It is evident from the above figures that in Kandlaguduru village, the strength of students was 45 in Class I and decreased to a figure as low as 21 in Class V, which is a decrease of more than 50 per cent. We found further deterioration in the case of girl students. As against 25 girl students in Class I, only 4 girls students were present in Class V. It was discovered that there as many as 111 children in the village who were not going to school.

The figures in the case of Mallenipalli village too indicate a large dropout rate of children. When compared to the strength of 45 in Class I, the strength in Class V was as low as 15. Most of the children that we saw, who were outside the school, were employed in cotton fields in this area.

Appecherla is an interior village. Here too the dropout rate was very high with most of the children engaged in cotton fields. Merchants and landlords come from the coastal district of Andhra Pradesh to engage

Table 3.2
Class-wise Distribution of Students in the School in Mallenipalli Village

Standard	Boys	Girls	Total
I	30	15	45
II	12	10	22
III	14	13	27
IV	13	11	24
V	9	6	15

Table 3.3
Comparison of Strength of Children Enrolled with Actual Attendance in the School in Appecherla Village

Standard	Strength of Children			Actual Attendance		
	Boys	Girls	Total	Boys	Girls	Total
I	40	29	69	33	20	53
II	47	40	87	28	34	62
III	19	7	26	11	5	16
IV	22	7	29	16	7	23
V	9	8	17	3	5	8

children for agricultural work on contract basis for about three to four months paying them a paltry sum of Rs 400 to Rs 500 a month.

The data in Table 3.3 gave us a glimpse of the high percentage of school dropouts. As against 69 children in Class I, the strength of enrolled students was down to a mere 17 in Class V. Figures that showed actual attendance were even more dismal. As against 53 children in Class I, only 8 were attending classes in Class V. Plagued by acute poverty, the children as well as their parents were lured by landlords and contractors who exploited the deprived and ignorant children for their own selfish purposes.

On interacting with teachers we discovered that interpolation exists in almost all the schools with the Government of India (GOI) implementing the 'Three Kg Rice Scheme'. Students who have 80 per cent attendance are provided 3 kg of rice by the government as a token of encouragement. But this scheme is very often misused as actual attendance is found to be at variance with the figures shown. Accordingly, we conducted a survey in six villages with specific focus on the 'Rice Scheme'.

We were curious to know whether children were really attending school or coming to collect their share of rice. Also, whether the children would dropout of school in case the scheme was to be discontinued or replaced by one in which they would be provided stationery items such as pens, pencils and erasers. Parents' opinion were also sought in this regard.

Table 3.4
Views of the Parents of Dimmagudi School Children on Attendance due to the Rice Scheme: A Sample Presentation

Name of the Child	Caste	Child's Attitude				Parents' Attitude			
		If rice scheme discontinued, will they continue studies		Will they prefer pen, pencil, rubbers, etc., in place of 3 kg of rice		If rice scheme discontinued, will they continue their children's studies		Will they prefer pen, pencil, rubbers, etc., in place of 3 kg of rice	
		Yes	No	Yes	No	Yes	No	Yes	No
M. Varalakshmi	SC	✓	–	✓	–	✓	–	✓	–
B. Padmavathi	SC	✓	–	✓	–	✓	–	✓	–
A. Narendra	SC	✓	–	✓	–	–	✓	–	✓
M. Pulirangadir	SC	–	✓	–	✓	–	✓	–	✓
A. Balachandra	SC	✓	–	✓	–	–	✓	✓	–
A. Ragendra	SC	✓	–	✓	–	✓	–	✓	–
M. Sudhir	SC	✓	–	✓	–	✓	–	✓	–
T. Ramamohan	SC	✓	–	✓	–	–	✓	–	✓
B. Rajesekhar	SC	✓	–	✓	–	✓	–	–	✓
S. Nageswaramma	SC	✓	–	✓	–	✓	–	–	✓

Figure 3.1
Views of the Parents of Dimmagudi School Children on Attendance due to the Rice Scheme: A Graphic Presentation

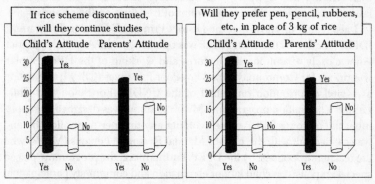

Figure 3.1 shows that children do not care for the rice scheme but parents insist on it.

The Public Report on Basic Education (PROBE) was yet another eye-opener, as it helped us to understand that almost all child labourers have a lot of free time.

Figure 3.2
How Out-of-School Children Spend a 12-hour Day

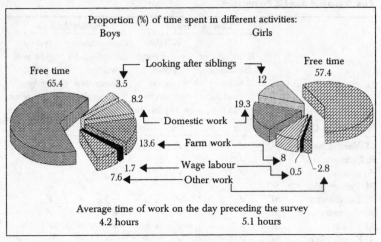

Proportion (%) of time spent in different activities:
Boys   Girls

Free time   Looking after siblings   Free time
65.4   3.5   12   57.4
                8.2   19.3
                        Domestic work
                13.6 ◄— Farm work
                1.7 ◄— Wage labour —► 8
                7.6 ◄————— Other work   0.5   2.8

Average time of work on the day preceding the survey
4.2 hours   5.1 hours

Source: The PROBE Team, 1999, 'Public Report on Basic Education in India', p. 29, New Delhi: Oxford university Press.

According to the survey described in Figure 3.2, children were not engaged in work throughout the year and employment was offered to them during the cropping and harvesting seasons. Thus, these child labourers were left with a fair amount of free time on their hands.

I also came to know that the District Primary Education Programme (DPEP) funded by the World Bank was operating in the Anantapur district. After closely examining the features and working of the DPEP, a plan was drawn for Community Based Pro-Poor Initiatives (CBPPI) to function as a vital contribution on behalf of the UNDP's Education and Child Labour Elimination programme. My programme was designed to supplement the ongoing DPEP while avoiding any manner of duplication and was carried out with the help of Mandal Resource Persons (MRPs) who are teachers appointed by the DPEP. Furthermore, the programme placed special emphasis on child labour elimination and community participation.

In brief, some salient features of the programme in contrast with the DPEP were:

1. The development of need-based training modules.
2. Monitoring registers that help to keep a close watch on the progress achieved.

3. An innovative method which involved the convergence of various government departments and ministries in order to expedite work and cut down on unnecessary expenses.
4. Emphasis on promoting a joyful method of learning through development with appropriate teaching material.
5. Facilitating the community to participate in the child labour programme.
6. Opening of residential camps for the successful rehabilitation of grown-up child labourers.

According to the DPEP figures, only a small number of 58 child labourers existed in the area of 20 villages. However, while touring the district we discovered hundreds of young children toiling in the quarries (*chinna gani* and *pedda gani*) of Kristipadu village, in the cotton fields of Mallenipalli and Appecherla, and the chilli fields of Kandlaguduru village. Thus, a fresh survey was conducted in a systematic manner. A new methodology and techniques specially devised for the purpose were constituted in order to get an exact picture of the number of child labourers in the area identified in our programme.

To begin with, it was decided to conduct an intensive survey of the situation in 20 villages of Peddavaduguru mandal on an experimental basis. As I had visited a few other agencies involved in eradication of child labour, this experience helped me in designing forms and mapping, and I was also greatly assisted by the MRPs. Forms and mapping were developed and tested before implementation.

A group of local people that included *sarpanches*, headmasters, teachers, anganwadi workers, self-help group members, Ekalavya volunteers and social activists were identified for imparting training, conducting the survey and gathering required information. Further, a training module on the survey was developed with the assistance of the MRPs. The aim was to sensitise trainees on the issue of child labour. The training module was prepared in both Telugu (the local language) and English.

Training camps of six days' duration were organised for 20 villages and the participants were trained to conduct door-to-door surveys. They were also taught how to make school and village maps using the Participatory Rural Appraisal (PRA) technique and maintain education registers comprising of Forms I and II developed for the purpose (given in Annexures 5.1 and 5.2 in the workbook).

The training was made flexible with entertaining games and other activities. The medium of street theatre was also employed in the training process and the Jana Vignana Vedika, a youth voluntary organisation, presented several plays under the able direction of their leader Srinu of Peddavaduguru mandal.

Data soon started pouring in and I, along with MRPs and village school teachers, spent a hot week of April 1999 consolidating the enormous data that we had received. This provided us with a clear picture of the situation in 20 villages of Peddavaduguru mandal, where 903 children were found to be working as labourers while government records showed a figure of 58 child labourers. In addition, we now had definite information with regard to children who were not in school either because they had never been enrolled or because they had dropped out at some point. Equipped thus with a detailed view of the situation, I was able to carefully plan future course of action for the child labour elimination programme.

Also, from the school mapping, a clear picture emerged and we became familiar with houses where children were not going to school. A high rate of child labour/dropout prevailed in the villages of the area where the survey was conducted (Table 3.5).

Table 3.5
Survey of Three Villages (Out of 20) where Child Labour was High

Village	Child Labour
Bheemunipalli	114
Kandlaguduru	111
Appecherla	141

It was found that in three villages namely Kristipadu, Dimmagudi and Appecherla a large number of small children were not going to the anganwadi (Table 3.6).

Table 3.6
Survey of Three Villages (Out of 20) where Large Number of Small Children are Out of the Anganwadi

S.No.	Village	Children Out of the Anganwadi
1	Kristipadu	53
2	Dimmagudi	48
3	Appecherla	41

After intensive field tours and door-to-door survey, a clear picture emerged, thus enabling us to take decisions in the child labour elimination programme (Table 3.7).

Table 3.7

'Door-to-Door' Survey Figures of Peddavaduguru Mandal (ATP)

S.No.	Village Name	Total Family Number	Total Population			Education Status of 3-14 years Children														
						Anganwadi						Primary School						Going to High School		
						Going			Not Going			Going			Not Going					
		Number	lation	Male	Female	Boys	Girls	Total	Boys	Girls	Total	Boys	Girls	Total	Boys	Girls	Total	Boys	Girls	Total
1	P. Kottalapalli	156	813	404	409	8	20	28	2	1	3	52	72	124	8	6	14	32	38	70
2	Appecherla	318	1697	878	819	0	0	0	19	22	41	111	90	201	69	72	141	40	28	68
3	Kandlaguduru	223	1074	559	515	10	12	22	14	10	24	107	76	183	57	54	111	32	16	48
4	G. Venkatampalli	252	993	532	461	44	31	75	1	1	2	79	62	141	2	1	3	33	22	55
5	Mallenipalli	153	826	428	398	25	19	44	0	2	2	57	39	96	24	25	49	22	16	38
6	Veerapalli	34	199	102	97	0	0	0	3	3	6	18	16	34	2	8	10	10	2	12
7	Rampuram	116	455	251	204	13	7	20	2	3	5	44	39	83	2	4	6	13	6	19
8	Konapuram	88	473	249	224	12	10	22	4	2	6	97	43	140	17	13	30	14	3	17
9	G. Anantapur	342	1310	705	605	33	25	58	0	0	0	164	91	255	10	6	16	50	32	82
10	Virupapuram	206	1039	543	496	34	22	56	5	4	9	90	89	179	23	20	43	33	8	41
11	Dimmagudi	409	1703	902	801	0	0	0	20	28	48	158	141	299	15	48	63	52	21	73
12	Chitturu	227	999	515	484	0	0	0	0	0	0	78	51	129	12	23	35	17	7	24
13	Kristipadu	200	929	494	435	0	0	0	28	24	52	95	51	146	25	48	73	27	6	33
14	Kondupalli	95	452	233	219	15	14	29	0	0	0	29	33	62	2	12	14	14	11	25
15	Chinnavaduguru	286	1337	701	636	20	24	44	10	5	15	127	81	208	17	55	72	0	0	0
16	Kasepalli	254	1441	780	661	0	0	0	0	0	0	104	86	190	9	15	24	36	20	56
17	C. Ramarajupalli	105	533	280	253	17	11	28	1	3	4	51	27	78	8	13	21	6	5	11
18	Bhimunipalli	223	1346	770	526	0	0	0	0	0	0	130	115	245	53	61	114	24	5	29
19	Muppalagooty	169	848	433	415	22	18	40	1	0	1	97	84	181	12	19	31	22	6	28
20	Miduthuru	–	–	–	–	29	11	40	0	0	0	149	110	259	16	17	33	12	4	16
	Grand Total	3,856	18,467	9,759	8,658	282	224	506	110	108	218	1,837	1,396	3,233	383	520	903	489	256	745

Note: Total 903 child labourers found in 20 villages of Peddavaduguru mandal.

1. Some rooms were required in few schools in the villages of Kristipadu, Konapuram, Chitrachedu, Kandlaguduru and Virupapuram in the Peddavaduguru mandal; and Melapuram, Kotnoor and Rachapalli villages in the Hindupur mandal, as Classes I to V were being taught in a single room.
2. Requirement of extra anganwadi centres in Dimmagudi, Kristi-padu and Appecherla so as to accomodate maximum children in the age-group of 3–5 years who were not a part of anganwadi centres.
3. As child labour was high, intensive community campaign was required to admit them for two months in 'Back to School' programme run by the Government of Andhra Pradesh.

We strived to streamline dropout and never enrolled children into formal education. We were not only able to ascertain the correct number of child labourers but also became aware of the causes for the widespread prevalence of the menace of child labour.

Causes of Child Labour

Various reasons can be attributed to the evils of child labour. A careful analysis of the problem reveals that the following factors are the major contributors for child labour.

Poverty

Poverty is an all-pervading social evil. It is the root cause of many ills and all social evils emanate from it. When the income of a family is insufficient to meet the needs of its members, parents are forced to send their children to work. Given a choice most parents would not like their children to work. The pressure to survive is the main cause. 'No Work, No Food'— This pathetic condition forces the parents to send their children to work.

Family Size

Even though there is considerable change in the attitude of the families and majority of the people adopt small family norms, there has not been any major change. A family which consists of six children is a normal scene in the rural areas. The needs of the family are dependent on the size of the family. When the need goes up, there is bound to be an increase in the expenditure. This leads to the burden of earning more which has to be borne by all the family members irrespective of age. Thus, this is when children get engaged in work.

LACK OF PARENTAL INTEREST

This is applicable largely in the rural areas. The rural folk who are away from areas better exposed to education are unaware of the benefits that literacy or education reaps. They do not have faith in the educational system. With this perception, they are bound to send their children for labour because in their opinion education has no practical use.

ECONOMIC CONSTRAINTS

Assuming that the members a family can earn their livelihood even without engaging children in work, they are taken aback when the question of spending on education arises. Education is not altogether free. One is required to buy books, uniforms and stationery. Added to this, sometimes tuition fee has to be paid. This means that the poor parents have to earn not only for survival but also to meet the expenses of their children's education. As per the assessment of the PROBE survey, a minimum of Rs 318 is incurred annually towards the education of one child per year.

If a family fails to earn enough, they are bound to discourage their children from studying.

POOR TEACHING STANDARDS

When the above are the contributing factors for either 'never enrolled children' or 'dropouts', this and the following are the factors responsible for 'push outs'.

Teachers require necessary teaching skills, which should vary depending on the need. Children with rural backgrounds are entirely different from the ones in the urban areas. A teacher should realise this and should make teaching more interesting. The retention rate of the pupils in the school (in rural areas) mostly depends on the skill of the teachers to make classes more interesting. They should avoid being mechanical in their routine and try to divert at frequent intervals. Playing games, telling moral stories and, at times, teaching vocational skills, if incorporated in the curriculum, will automatically enhance the interest of children in schools.

CURRICULUM

This is also a factor which is responsible for 'push outs'. Curriculum should be set taking greater care. Lengthy, monotonous chapters discourage a child. Research in this aspect is necessary. Proper curriculum that will hold the attention and interest of children, which will also be useful for their future, is required.

DISTANCE

In rural areas, the schools are in most cases at a great distance from home. It is not surprising that children walk or cycle 10–20 kilometres a day to attend school. This proves as a discouraging factor. Girl students, especially, are prone to dropout as a result of distance.

INFRASTRUCTURE

In villages, most of the schools have two or three rooms. It is difficult to run two to three classes simultaneously in one room. Lack of infrastructure also leads to increase in the dropout rate and subsequently to the increase in child labour.

INADEQUATE TEACHERS

In rural areas every village school has two to three teachers in the primary schools. Lack of teaching staff also leads to children dropping out.

After training the *sarpanches*, headmasters, teachers, anganwadi workers, self-help groups, Ekalavya volunteers and activists, the stage was now set for community mobilisation. As mentioned earlier, it was felt that community participation was essential for successfully universalisation of elementary education.

COMMUNITY MOBILISATION

Community mobilisation is a pre-requisite for the eradication of child labour. The survey of the number of children employed as labourers in Anantapur district was completed on 10 April 1999. Looking at the data gathered, it was clear that we had a massive problem on our hands. Our primary task was to withdraw the children from the work sites and get them started on the process of achieving literacy. Since the child labourers were either illiterate or only semi-literate, their direct admission into village schools was entirely out of the question. A feasible alternative, ideally suited to the needs and conditions of such children was the Andhra Pradesh government's 'Back-to-School' programme that would in a period of two months prepare the children sufficiently to gain admission into regular schools or hostels. However, all this meant confronting the contractors as well as convincing the children and their parents. Thus commenced our campaign for community mobilisation.

Although, initially I had taken up three mandals—Gandlapenta, Peddavaduguru and Hindupur—all three of them were in three different directions. So for practical reasons, I decided to drop Gandlapenta.

The following villages were visited for the purpose of community mobilisation in the Peddavaduguru mandal—Chinnavaduguru, Dimmagudi, Muppalagooty, G. Venkatampalli, Kandlaguduru, Miduthuru, Kristipadu, Chitrachedu, Chitturu, C. Ramarajupalli, Rampuram, Gopurajupalli, Virupapuram, G. Anantapur, Ravuludiki, Konapuram, Bheemunipalli, Mallenipalli, Lakshumpalli, Appecherla, Kondupalli, Kasepalli, Veerepalli, Peddavaduguru and P. Kottalapalli.

In the Hindupur mandal, the villages that were visited were Rachepalli, Chalivendala, Gollapuram, Melapuram, Kotnoor, Thumakunta and Kotipi.

A unique feature of the community mobilisation programme surfaced in the form of participation of women belonging to self-help groups—a fine illustration of the force and strength spelt by women's empowerment. UNDP's *Human Development Report*[1] clearly brings out the role of women's empowerment for fostering economic growth and development:

> Investing in women's capabilities and empowering them to exercise their choices is not only valuable in itself but is also the surest way to contribute to economic growth and development.

Since women groups from UNDP and DWCRA were involved in the programme, it was felt that it would be a good idea to make our entry into the ranks of the community by attending meetings of the women's self-help groups (SHGs). The SHGs regularly meet and take participatory decisions on various issues including thrift and credit. All the SHGs in a

1. UNDP, 1995, *Human Development Report*. New York: Oxford University Press.

village federate into a village organisation. Different village organisations in a mandal, in turn, combine to form a Mandal Mahila Samakhya. The SHGs use the collected money to offer loans to members in need, thus enabling the women to not only escape from the clutches of unscrupulous moneylenders but also imbibe in them a sense of self-reliance.

Mobilisation was thus initiated through the SHGs. Village organisation meetings were usually held at night to make it convenient for the villagers to attend (as most of them go out to work during the day). The assistance of youth and women's groups was sought to prepare community charts containing information on the educational status of children of the respective villages as well as to arrange 'grama sabhas'. These 'grama sabhas' discuss problems of the village and also identify beneficiaries for the welfare schemes of the government. Besides members of women and youth groups, mandal education team members, local teachers, *sarpanches* and headmasters with other eminent members of the village community attended the 'grama sabhas'. Records regarding children who had never enrolled were available with the SHGs. Community charts were used in the meetings to discuss the problem of children who were not in school and, further, how such children could be streamlined into formal learning centres. Parents with children who either stayed back at home or went out to work were persuaded by the other members to send their wards to school. Door-to-door campaigns and rallies were also organised to mobilise community support and involvement. The participation on the part of the villagers was voluntary and enthusiastic. The subsequent creation of awareness in the community made our movement an extremely cost-effective one.

The importance of women in the development process became all too clear to me in the course of the community mobilisation campaign. A unique feature of this was the active support and participation of women especially from the SHGs. MMS leaders, like Aruna from Hindupur and Gurramma from Peddavaduguru, were most helpful when they came to know that I was there to work for the elimination of child labour and extended all possible assistance. In fact, it was at their behest that all the women leaders of the village organisation volunteered to have lists of 'out of school' children prepared. A group of women from G. Venkatampalli village of Peddavaduguru mandal also helped us by bringing 21 children from their village to join school. We were further encouraged when the women leaders invited us to visit each of their villages to create awareness through community mobilisation. At the village too, women evinced keen interest in seeing their children get decent education and were often found to persuade the men to accept the advantages of educating their children.

When I think of the help extended by the village women, the names of Obulamma and Achamma of Chinnavaduguru village from the Peddavaduguru mandal immediately come to mind. Both women worked hard to round up all the children of their village who had not enrolled and who were dropouts when we arrived there for the meeting.

Meeting with women self-help groups

Meanwhile, the 'Back-to-School' programme was to commence shortly leaving us with just 10 days to successfully complete the process of mobilisation. Inspite of all the assistance and cooperation extended by the women folk, I felt dissatisfied and feared that we had failed to reach out to the entire population of both mandals. Hence, it was decided that in villages where the incidence of child labour was relatively high, we would launch a 'door-to-door' campaign. In this regard, we requested the village teachers to use school mapping and provide us with lists. Equipped with these, we finally started by campaigning door-to-door in the village of Chinnavaduguru. The results were amazing. We met the child labourers, their parents and interacted with them in their own homes, which proved efficacious in winning them over. The response was so overwhelming that after visiting just four homes, the villagers took over and went to each and every house repeating each word that we had spoken with equal conviction.

INVOLVEMENT OF TEACHERS IN CAMPAIGNING

School teachers in the area, brought together under the aegis of the Bal Karmika Vimochana Vedika (BKVV), a teachers' union, also participated in the community mobilisation campaign. As a matter of fact, the presence of the teachers at village organisation meetings and the door-to-door campaign helped to bring them closer to the community. At every village, the school teachers, the principals along with MRPs—Sudhakar and Narayana Swamy in Peddavaduguru mandal and Ramakrishna and Shyamala in Hindupur mandal—accompanied me. Door-to-door campaign was thus successfully carried out in the villages of Miduthuru, Kristipadu, Kandlaguduru, Chinnavaduguru and Lakshumpalli. On 20 April 1999, just as I was preparing to make a night halt at Kristipadu, I received the news that one of my family members had passed away. I was faced with a painful dilemma. On the one hand, my presence at home was clearly needed and, on the other hand, I had promised to visit three villages the same day, and if I did not do so, the sentiments of the simple trusting villagers would be hurt. Fortunately, District Girl Child Development Officer (DGCDO), Vijayalakshmi came to my aid. She, along with APC/DPEP Jayaram, took my place in the campaign during the two days of my absence. On 22 April 1999, I resumed my campaign.

CONTRIBUTION OF THE YOUTH

The youth of the villages must also be commended in making our campaign a success. I approached youth groups of the villages known as Jana Vignana Vedika (JVV) and persuaded them to work for our cause of spreading awareness and thus mobilising the community. The village youth worked hard and sincerely during the entire campaign without accepting any form of compensation. The momentum gained by the movement was sufficient to inspire these young people. They took training in the form of spreading awareness among the masses and in developing a scientific temper through education and cultural activities. In Peddavaduguru, the JVV staged plays to mobilise child labourers as well as their parents.

Youth groups

CHILD TO CHILD APPROACH

Children were themselves willing to campaign for the programme. Especially in the Dimmagudi child labour residential camp of Peddavaduguru mandal, it was found that the 'child to child' campaign was extremely fruitful. Nagi Reddy, the headmaster of the Z.P. School, Dimmagudi instructed his high school children to mobilise dropouts or never enrolled child labourers from their respective villages. These efforts resulted in many child labourers, including contract labourers, joining the Dimmagudi child labour residential camp.

The community mobilisation campaign was successful in many ways but had some problematic moments too. I was once stopped near the village Chitturu of Peddavaduguru mandal by three naxalites and questioned about the role of the UNDP project. Before I could even begin to explain, the angry men started berating me. I heard them out in silence mainly because I lacked fluency in Telugu. This proved to be to my advantage as the men felt that I was listening to them patiently and without resistance. I was, however, never again bothered by any naxalites during my entire stay in the district.

There was also some trouble caused by local drunkards. In some villages, it is not unusual to find some men drunk after sunset. One day, near Muppalagooty village, three men who were in a state of inebriation stopped me and asked me for money. Being alone at that time, I handed over the sum I was carrying without any protest. At the Kotipi village in Hindupur mandal, one night, a few drunkards tried to disturb our meeting, but the women present there drove them away. The strength and courage of the women was truly amazing.

Yet another tense situation comes to mind which took place in Racha-palli village of the Hindupur mandal. We were with women's groups discussing problems and strategies, when a woman approached me with tears in her eyes. On being asked what the matter was, the woman replied that she wanted her son, a contract labourer, to be educated. We approached the women's groups for their help. The group leaders immediately offered to give a loan of the sum required to be paid for the release of the boy. However, they were afraid to approach the contractor. We met the contractor, Chandrasekhar, who agreed to release the boy if the amount due to him was paid, but later he went back on his word. Later that night, as we were preparing to leave after our meeting, Chandrasekhar, accompanied by other labour contractors, confronted us shouting that we could never eliminate child labour.

One of the project functionaries tried to sensitise the contractors but in vain. I then intervened and invited the them to come into the school for discussions.

On hearing my words spoken in Telugu—'Nenu oka vinnapam chep-pan?' (Can I make a request?), the contractors softened in their attitude and agreed to listen to what I had to say. I quietly enquired whether their own children were attending school. When they replied in the affirmative, I simply asked, 'If so, why not give Gangadri a chance too?' Speechless and ashamed, the contractors calmed down and Chandrasekhar agreed to release Gangadri after receiving the money that was due to him.

Thus, with the hard work and cooperation from our team members, women's groups, the local youth and village school children, we were able to complete the community mobilisation campaign successfully. At the time of the 'Back to School' programme, we had about 1,000 child labourers, illiterate as well as semi-literate, who were eager to join the programme and gain at least elementary education. The beginning of a breakthrough could faintly be seen in the distant horizon.

BACK TO SCHOOL

SYNOPTIC VIEW OF THE 'BACK TO SCHOOL' PROGRAMME

The 'Back to School'[2] programme is run by the Department of Social Welfare, Government of Andhra Pradesh. The duration of the course is for two months. This programme is aimed at coaching and streamlining children who are classified into two categories, school dropouts and children who have never been enrolled.

The main aim is to motivate and rope in illiterate and semi-literate children, who were working as labourers, into schools depending on their age, their capacity to learn and desire to attain the required academic standards.

ENROLMENT OF CHILDREN

The occurrence of child labour is very high in Anantapur district. All the child labourers are either totally illiterate or semi-literate (dropout children can be classified as semi-literate).

After protracted canvassing and mobilisation, many children were admitted in Peddavaduguru and Hindupur hostels. With the help of activists and other volunteers, it was possible to admit more than a 1,000 children. However, on careful screening it was found that some of them were regularly attending their village schools and such children were removed from the hostels. By the end of this exercise of identification and the shifting process, 585 children joined the Peddavaduguru hostel and 352 joined the Hindupur hostel. Most of the children were child labourers around the age of 6 years onwards. As the number of enrolled children was high, there was a great deal of difficulty in not only handling them but also sustaining their interest. It was further discovered that the volunteers who were in charge of the two-month course were not

---

2. The State of Andhra Pradesh has the highest number of child workers in the country. A large proportion of the child labourers belong to the Scheduled Caste/Scheduled Tribe community. In order to reach these deprived children, the Government of Andhra Pradesh initiated a pilot programme 'Back to School' in all the 23 districts of the state. It is run in social welfare hostels (meant for the Scheduled Castes) for two months during summer vacations. After two months' intensive coaching, efforts are made to streamline child labour into regular schools/hostels.

competent enough to handle such children. The importance of providing training to the volunteers and upgrading their skills was felt. Hence, efforts were made to prepare a training module and train the volunteers in effective teaching methods. In this training module, stress was laid on the 'Joyful Method of Learning' including, among other things, '*Aata, Maata, Patta*' (play, speech and songs), to ensure that the interest of the children was sustained.

DETAILS OF THE 'BACK TO SCHOOL' PROGRAMME, 1999

The main reasons for dropout/never enrolled children in Anantapur district have been identified in Figure 3.3.

One day, I was returning to Peddavaduguru from Kristipadu village around 9:30 p.m. The women's group had just concluded their meeting and were about to disperse when I reached Peddavaduguru. I was surprised to find that at the Centre for the 'Back to School' programme, gates were open and many people had gathered outside their houses.

Child labourers at Kristapadu
(175 of them joined 'Back to School' programme)

I was curious to know the reason behind this. I found out that a young girl was vomiting. She looked very ill and was sitting in the lap of her weeping, distraught mother. I was told Kullayamma had been bitten by a mad dog. Vaccine was not available in the village and the girl was not only running high temperature but was also vomiting continuously. On an impulse, I picked up the girl and, along with her mother, started for

Figure 3.3

Pictorial Presentation of Common Factors Identified for Child Labour in 20 Villages

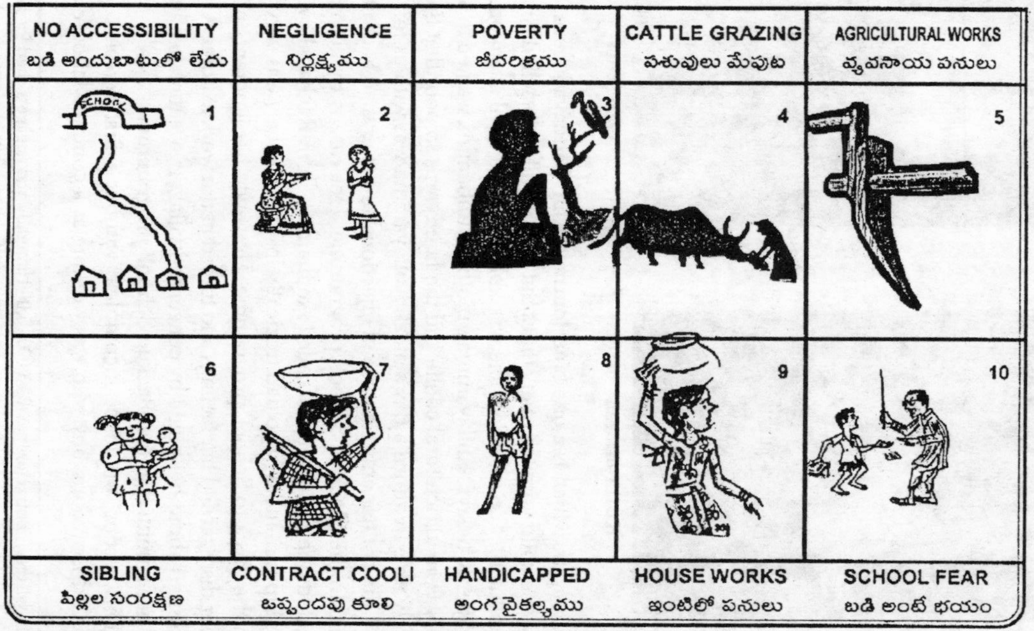

NO ACCESSIBILITY
బడి అందుబాటులో లేదు
NEGLIGENCE
నిర్లక్ష్యము
POVERTY
బీదరికము
CATTLE GRAZING
పశువులు మేపుట
AGRICULTURAL WORKS
వ్యవసాయ పనులు
SCHOOL
1
2
3
4
5
6
7
8
9
10
SIBLING
పిల్లల సంరక్షణ
CONTRACT COOLI
ఒప్పందపు కూలి
HANDICAPPED
అంగ వైకల్యము
HOUSE WORKS
ఇంటిలో పనులు
SCHOOL FEAR
బడి అంటే భయం

Note: Sketches developed with the help of a local youth at Paddavaduguru.

Kullayamma   **Gangadri**

Anantapur, which is a one hour journey from Peddavaduguru. On our way, the child vomited many times but held on till we reached Anantapur at about 10.30 p.m. where she was able to get medical attention.

After two days, Kullayamma's mother Subbamma wanted to leave, as she was an agricultural coolie and the family was so poor that they were barely able to afford a day's meal. Kullayamma was with us for 12 days until she got her entire course of injections and after that, I admitted her again in the 'Back to School' programme. Her case is by no means an isolated one. Another girl, called Anjinamma from Rachapalli village of Hindupur mandal (who had tragically lost her mother) was very keen to join the 'Back to School' programme. However, her ignorant and selfish father disregarded her feelings and forced her to work at home. On being informed about her plight by concerned villagers, we took her away and got her admitted in the 'Back to School' programme.

This section would be incomplete without a first person report by Gangadri, a young boy who was working as a contract[3] labourer.

---

3. In villages, contractors pay Rs 3,000–5,000 annually and engage a child for 12 months. In return, this child has to carry out not only fieldwork but also attend to household chores and stay with the contractor. It was observed that villagers call this contract/ bonded labour. However, as per law, it is different from contract/bonded labour. A brief description about the Contract Labour Act and Bonded Labour Act is given in Annexure 14.1 of the workbook.

I am a 13 year old Scheduled Caste boy from the Rachapalli village of Hindupur mandal. My parents are agricultural labourers. I have two elder sisters who are married. My elder brother has been a contract labourer for 6 years and now he works as an agricultural labourer. I have three younger brothers too.

All my younger brothers are studying. However, due to poverty and my sisters' marriages, we (the elder brothers) had to continue working as contract labourers. In April 1999, when the UNDP Consultant and Project Officer came to our village, my mother and father were really convinced by their reasoning. They wanted me to join school but were scared to approach Chandrasekhar (a landlord and my contractor). My mother is a member of a self-help group and the members of her group agreed to advance her a loan to get me released from the landlord's clutches. The UNDP Consultant approached my landlord and at first he protested saying that 'UNDP cannot erase the system of child labour'. The UNDP Consultant then reasoned with the landlord arguing that education was essential to all children and every child had a right to study in the same way as his own children. The landlord was convinced and finally he relented. I was thrilled! I had been working so hard all the day in the fields, taking cattle for grazing in the hot sun, attending to household chores and sleeping late at night. There was never any time for rest or play. When my landlord's children went to school in school uniforms and shining shoes, I used to look at them feeling dejected.

Finally, I joined the 'Back to School' programme. I am very happy today because the hot sun no longer bothers me and learning through playing and singing is great fun. After completing the bridge course, I joined the social welfare hostel at Chilamattur and I am both excited and contented about my future. I am in the third standard and my younger brother who is in the sixth standard is helping me cope with my studies. The 'Back to School' programme not only gave me education, it also gave me a chance to experience the brighter side of life.

When the Governors of Andhra Pradesh and Karnataka paid a visit to the child labour camp, I was given Rs 6,000 from the Venkamma Memorial as prize. This amount has been invested in Monthly Income Scheme (MIS) and I get Rs 60 per month. I am happy that I was rescued from the clutches of the contractor and the drudgery and I also got monetary help which will help me in continuing my education. Seeing me progress well in studies, three more contract labour boys from my village have been admitted in the hostel.

This statement itself sums up the programme more than anything else. In the final analysis, Anantapur was one of the districts which exceeded its target (Table 3.8).

Table 3.8

*Social Welfare Department 'Back to School' Programme during 1999
in Anantapur District*

	No. of Centres		No. of Students
Target	97		9,700
Achieved	98		10,873
UNDP Adopted Mandals*	Boys	Girls	Total
Peddavaduguru	315	270	585
Hindupur	250	102	352
Total	565	372	937

Note: * In these two mandals a large number of Scheduled Caste child labourers were
mobilised.

The Chief Minister of Andhra Pradesh, Shri Nara Chandra Babu Naidu
evinced keen interest in the programme during his visit to one of the
social welfare hostels conducting the 'Back to School' programme for
girls in the Hindupur mandal of Anantapur district. The Chief Minister
was impressed when the children present at the camp displayed their
progress by narrating all that they had learnt. He was visibly pleased and
commented that all the girls looked bright and cheerful. The girls in
chorus expressed their desire to continue their studies in the future. The
Chief Minister was not only satisfied with the cleanliness, maintenance
and hygienic conditions at the social welfare hostel but also with the confidence expressed by these young girls. On request by the Deputy Director
of Social Welfare, he sanctioned Rs 20 lakh for the social welfare
department of Anantapur district.

The district officials monitored the progress and functioning of the
hostel, the District Collector personally paid surprise visits to test the
quality of food served as well as the behaviour of the volunteers towards
the children.

After the basic objective of the programme was met and the residential
school had been running for two months, a number of working children
were withdrawn from their work environment. The entire thrust was to
prepare them for a transition to the formal school system. The process
bridging was found particularly useful with older children who had been
working for sometime, for it provided them the scope to enter into appropriate grades in the formal school. However, there were lots of hurdles
which had to be tackled with presence of mind. For example, during
study hours, especially at night, children were unable to concentrate on

Chief Minister N. Chandra Babu Naidu with girl child labourers of one of the hostels, conducting 'Back to school' programme at Anantapur district

their studies due to constant power cuts. This was tackled by providing solar lights. After determined collective efforts, exams were conducted, and subsequently, all the children were admitted in regular schools and hostels.

PERRAMMA'S EXPERIENCE WITH THE
'BACK TO SCHOOL' PROGRAMME

Perramma, a woman leader, was of immense help when it came to community mobilisation. Basically from the village of G. Venkatampalli, Perramma talks about her experience of working with us:

> From the very beginning I was associated with this programme. I am a group leader representing my village. In the past I tried to help many women from the weaker sections and encouraged them to form self-help groups. I learnt a lot about the UNDP project and got interested in the child labour elimination programme. We were successful in streamlining 21 children into the 'Back to School' programme.
>
> I was even made the chief guest for the inaugural programme. These 21 children completed the two-month programme and joined Gooty BC hostel.

In the past we were not aware of the existing educational facilities. Today we are active participants. We share good rapport with the MRPs, especially Sudhakar Babu and Narayanswamy. Sometimes we discuss the problems we face in the local schools with them. The child labour elimination programme has brought the teachers closer to our community. Personally, I have gained love, respect and support in my village. It gives me a lot of happiness to see our children finally in the sphere of education. We have benefited immensely from this project.

EXPERIENCES OF KULLAYA REDDY AND UMA MAHESWARA REDDY

Kullaya Reddy is eight years old. On completing the 'Back to School' course at Peddavaduguru, he is presently studying in Class II at the Social Welfare BC Boys Hostel at Gooty. He has shown immense progress in his studies. Perhaps the determination has come from the hard life he has lived. His mother was killed while working in the fields. Kullaya has an elder brother, Uma Maheswara, who is also studying with him. After the death of their mother both the children moved to Konduru village along with their father. However, due to faction rivalry, a case was registered against their father. The father went to jail, and it was at this time that we approached these two boys. Before they joined the 'Back to School'

The brothers, Kullaya and Uma Maheswara

programme, both the brothers had to work very hard. Their work included cattle grazing, carrying heavy loads at quarries and attending to domestic chores in exchange for food. Today, these boys are happy and relieved to be a part of the residential camp. They say: 'We have never been happier! Our good days have finally come. Today we have people who truly care for us.' Not only are they happy but have become goal-oriented. Kullaya wants to become a doctor while Uma Maheswara hopes to become an engineer.

At the end of the 'Back to School' programme, we could get 250 children admitted in different government hostels run by the social welfare/ ST welfare/BC welfare departments.

Back to School at Peddavaduguru

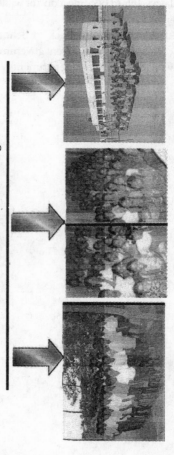

BC Gooty Boys Hostel

BC Gooty Girls Hostel

Peddavaduguru Hostel

CHAPTER 4

TOWARDS A BETTER LIFE:
SOME SOLUTIONS

BRIDGE COURSES

Despite the fact that 250 children were admitted in government hostels, we found that there were still some children who were unable to find a place in the government hostels. In order to accommodate such children, we planned to start bridge course centres in the villages where incidence of child labour was high.

The main thrust of the child labour rehabilitation project in Anantapur district was to enable the dropouts and illiterate children acquire some form of elementary education. We felt that this could be achieved by Andhra Pradesh government's 'Back to School' programme. Based on this objective, we were able to streamline almost 250 children out of approximately 1,000 who had joined for admission into the Social Welfare, Backward Class and Scheduled Tribe Welfare hostels in various places like Gooty, Peddavaduguru, Hindupur and Chilamathuru. However, as the number of such hostels in the district were few (in relation to the large number of child labourers), many children were not able to find a place and as a consequence they were admitted to the village schools.

This created a severe problem of adjustment. Cases were encountered where the child labourers were put in elementary schools in their respective villages. Most of the children could not easily accept the fact that they had to start with the lowest class. It meant learning with children younger than themselves. Consequently, many children opted out and went back to work. Furthermore, we felt that some of the children who had never been inside the portals of a school in all their lives would be able to cope academically only if they were provided with some extra coaching. Thus, with such support, an eight-year old could be expected to come up from zero level to Class III in just one year.

It was at this juncture that the National Project Coordinator suggested that bridge course centres[1] be set up in villages with a high incidence of child labour. These centres were to enable a child to make up for the lost years and in a shorter time make his/her entry into the village school in a class rightly suited for his/her age. The main aim of a bridge course centre, therefore, was to help the older illiterate children pass at least two classes in a year so that they did not have to face the embarrassment of having to study in a class with children younger to them. Such fast pace learning was absolutely necessary if the children were to be dissuaded from returning to work.

A visit was made to the Rishi Valley School in Madanapalli (in the Chittoor district of Andhra Pradesh) with the hope of gaining some other insights on this issue. Rishi Valley has satellite schools where children learn to read, write and unleash their creativity in a joyful environment.

The school has developed a kit to ensure that children find the learning process truly enjoyable. I got one of these kits, and it was decided that some features which we thought might be useful for our children would be adopted.

We also visited the Mamidipudi Venkatarangaiah Foundation which runs several bridge course centres but were told that they did not have any standard material and they develop curriculum along with the students drawing from their experiences. It was finally decided that we would develop our own bridge course material for our centres. So a brainstorming session was held with six Mandal Resource Persons (MRPs). We worked hard from morning till late at night discussing ideas, proposals and designing writing material that could be used to help the newly inducted children. We hoped that this would bridge the gap in their learning process and help them catch up with other children of their own age-group studying in local schools. In a week's time, we were able to bring out three books that would help the children to bridge the gap till Class III, so that they could be streamlined into formal schooling. Care was taken to ensure that the material developed entail simple teaching methods and also served to make learning a joyful experience for the children. This was followed by selection of paper, printing, designing of the cover and other related

---

1. In villages, the number of teachers is inadequate and sometime vacancies also exist. Child labourers after the two-month 'Back to School' programme need extra coaching so that they can bridge the education gap and come to the requisite standard. Hence, extra teachers are required exclusively for these child labourers, who are known as bridge course teachers. This course is run in the village schools and child labourers in the age-group of 6–9 years are admitted.

Books developed for the bridge courses

activities. Thus, in a short period of time (i.e., 9–14 June 1999) we were successful in bringing out three books on subjects like mathematics, environmental science and Telugu for our bridge course centres.

It must be pointed out here that all this was accomplished at an amazing speed only because every ounce of talent was tapped through motivation of each member in the team. The six MRPs were so highly charged with energy and enthusiasm that at times it became difficult to keep pace with them.

The next task was to select villages where our centres were urgently needed. On the basis of survey reports and 'Back to School' figures of the respective villages in the district, it was decided to open 26 centres in Peddavaduguru mandal and 27 centres in Hindupur mandal where the incidence of the highest dropout rate of child labourers was more. To be more specific, the presence of a minimum of 20 child labourers in a village was taken as the main criterion for having a bridge course centre. It was felt that the village school teachers were overburdened and would not be able to do justice if given the additional responsibility. Hence, we decided to appoint one bridge course volunteer/teacher for each centre to streamline the children who were never enrolled and dropout child labourers (between the age of 6–9).

In order to select teachers, we requested the local youth to talk to young men and women in the villages who had passed the intermediate examination but were unemployed. The *sarpanches* were also of great assistance in the area of mobilising unemployed youth to work as volunteers in our centres. The response was good, even though it was sad to see that some of the villages did not have even a single youth who qualified as a volunteer. At the time of the interview and selection, we especially looked for a sense of dedication and self-motivation together with the willingness to work hard in the candidates. Care was also taken to select people from the very same villages where the centres were set up. This was to ensure that the bridge course teachers could hold evening classes for the local children besides keeping an eye on their general welfare.

A week-long training was imparted to the selected teachers with the help of visuals which dealt with the three books developed by us and by using the Rishi Valley kit. Emphasis was laid on a more creative method of teaching, which would, in turn, lead to a joyful process of learning. The teachers were trained to bring the children up by one class each in about four to five months.

The next problem we had to grapple with was the matter of space that the bridge course centres had to operate from. The existing village schools had little room to spare and more often the bridge course classes had to be conducted in the open, under the trees. Construction of bridge course rooms took place at Virupapuram, G. Anantapuram, Gooty-Venkatampalli, Lakshumpalli in Peddavaduguru mandal and Kotnoor, Melapuram and Rachapalli in the Hindupur mandals with the help of funds from the MPLADS given by the Anantapur MPs.

Bridge Course Room, Kotnoor, Hindupur

However, we soon discovered some serious flaws in the way the courses were being conducted. This was largely due to the fact that in spite of our careful selection procedure, not all the volunteers were dedicated to the task they were entrusted with. A careful study of the problem and its possible causes revealed that the main reason was the casual attitude of the teachers. First, a complete lack of monitoring of the work being done in the bridge course centres together with lack of accountability on the part of the volunteers led to a drastic decline in teaching standards in many cases. The problem was aggravated by the low monetary benefits offered. Further, it was felt that the bridge course teachers feared that they might lose their jobs if all child labourers were streamlined. This led to a deliberate attempt to slow down the process and hang on to their only means of livelihood. Measures to rectify the situation were resorted to immediately. The bridge course teachers were made to report to the principals of their respective village schools. This was to ensure that local monitoring was done. Further, the principals were instructed to avail the special facilities available at the bridge course centres by admitting academically weak or slow children. This was to enable such children to benefit from the special attention given and the volunteers in the bridge course centres to find a new sense of security. This was to assure them that their utility was not confined merely to the short-term project of streamlining the child labourers.

A remarkable improvement in the working of the bridge course centres was noticed soon after some of the abovementioned corrective measures were taken. The process of streamlining the child labourers and preparing them to gradually merge into the formal academic stream progressed satisfactorily with the volunteers displaying a renewed spirit and vigour. Altogether 824 child labourers joined the bridge course at Hindupur and 566 joined at Peddavaduguru mandal (a sample of the Hindupur mandal details are shown in Table 4.1).

Table 4.1
Bridge Course Particulars–Hindupur

			Number of Child Labourers							
S. No.	Name of the Volunteer	Name of the Village	As per Survey			Admitted			Main Streamed		
			B	G	T	B	G	T	B	G	T
UNDP Centres (in the villages)											
1	K. Phani Kumar	C. Cherlopalli	10	12	22	11	12	23	5	5	10
2	E. Hari Prasad	Balamapalli	15	10	25	9	9	13	6	3	9
3	P.N. Sunil Kumar	Chalivendala	18	12	30	10	9	19	2	2	4
4	P.T. Govind Raj	Meenakuntapalli	10	15	25	10	8	18	6	3	9
5	S. Radha	Malugur	20	19	39	16	11	27	9	5	14
6	G. Ramanjineyulu	Nandamuri Nagar	16	16	32	11	16	27	4	4	8
7	D. Sujatha	M. Beerapalli	14	14	28	12	12	24	6	7	13
8	D. Jayalakshmi	C. Guddampalli	6	14	20	5	13	18	2	5	10
9	G. Subbi Reddy	Subbireddi Palli	13	17	30	11	16	27	5	9	14
10	N. Bhaskar Reddy	Kotnur	12	9	21	5	10	15	5	8	13
11	N. Sreenivasulu	Pulakunta	15	15	30	3	10	13	3	7	10

(contd)

(contd)

S. No.	Name of the Volunteer	Name of the Village	As per Survey B	G	T	Admitted B	G	T	Main Streamed B	G	T
12	M. Ganarasimha Murthy	Chowlur	15	12	27	11	8	19	2	1	3
13	U. Jabeer	Gollapuram	10	16	26	4	9	13	3	4	7
14	A. Ramanji	do	8	15	23	3	11	14	Closed		
15	T. Nagamani	Checkpost Colony	6	10	16	4	8	12	2	4	6
16	K.V. Aruna Jyothi	Mittameedapalli	10	10	20	6	7	13	2	3	5
17	G. Gangadevi	K.W. Colony	12	15	27	6	12	18	6	9	15
18	V. Sreenivasulu	N.T.R. Colony	10	16	26	8	12	18	6	9	15
19	L. Ramanjinappa	Prashanth Nagar	16	16	32	10	12	22	7	6	13
20	C.T. Manjula	Ambedkar Nagar	18	22	30	9	16	25	6	9	15
21	K. Shobha	do	14	18	32	10	11	21	5	6	11
22	K. Sathyanarayana	Nethaji Nagar	20	12	32	10	14	24	9	12	21
23	S. Dadapeer	Thyagaraja Nagar	18	21	39	10	12	22	6	6	12
24	M. Thulasi	do	12	18	30	7	15	22	4	9	13
25	L.N. Anitha	do	22	24	46	11	14	25	5	5	10
26	H. Narasimhappa	Melapuram HW	16	20	36	9	13	22	4	4	8
27	N. Aswathamma	do	17	22	39	12	16	28	3	3	6
28	H.S. Gangabhavani	do	12	14	28	6	12	18	3	3	6
29	C. Ratjna	do U.P.	14	18	32	9	12	21	3	7	10
	Total		399	452	851	248	340	588	131	160	291
DPEP Centres											
1	K. Pradeep Kumar	Chalivendala	20	16	36	7	13	20	5	3	8
2	S.P. Lakshmi	Malugur	16	16	32	6	15	21	6	7	13
3	K. Raveendra Reddy	Kotnur	18	13	31	15	10	25	6	3	9
4	D. Sathyavathi	Manesamudram	18	15	33	15	12	27	6	5	11
5	B. Manjula	Rachapalli	11	17	28	8	14	22	6	7	13
6	C. Sunandamma	Pulakunta	18	24	42	11	19	30	3	2	5
7	B.H. Rathanam Pille	Thumakunta	12	15	27	9	11	20	4	2	6
8	N.A. Kamla	Santhebidaur	10	22	32	3	18	21	4	16	20
9	H. Bhagyamma	Applakunta	11	16	27	7	11	18	5	5	10
10	M.V.K. Rishnaveni	Kotipi	20	18	38	2	10	12	2	7	9
11	S. Sanjeevarayappa	Bevinahalli	12	18	30	4	16	20	2	5	7
	Total		166	190	356	87	149	236	49	62	111
	Mandal grand total		565	642	1,207	335	489	824	180	222	402

Note: B—Boys; G—Girls; T—Total.

Meanwhile, the DPEP talked of plans to set up additional bridge courses. Aware that my tenure in the district as the National Consultant was drawing to an end and satisfied with the smooth running of our bridge course centres, I coordinated with the DPEP and handed over the UNDP centres to them in December 1999. Thus, not only was the programme that had started in Anantapur sustained but vital links with government departments were also established.

Bridge course centres were established at:

Peddavaduguru Mandal

1. Virupapuram
2. Chinnavaduguru
3. Goparajpalli
4. Miduthuru-1
5. Miduthuru-2
6. Chitrachedu
7. Rampuram
8. Chitturu
9. G. Anantapur
10. Dimmagudi
11. Mallenipalli
12. Lakshumpalli
13. P. Kottalapalli
14. Kandlaguduru
15. Ravuludiki
16. Bheemunipalli-1
17. Bheemunipalli-2
18. Konapuram
19. Appecherla
20. Gooty-Venkatampalli
21. C. Ramarajupalli
22. Lakshumpalli (NFE)
23. Chinnavaduguru (NFE)
24. Peddavaduguru (NFE)
25. Mallenipalli (NFE)
26. Gooty-Venkatampalli

Hindupur Mandal

1. Gollapuram
2. Chalivendala
3. Meenakuntapalli
4. C. Guddampalli
5. N.T.R. Colony
6. Gollapuram
7. Nethaji Nagar
8. Ambedkar Nagar
9. Chalivendala
10. Meenakuntapalli
11. C. Guddampalli
12. Chowlur
13. Gollapuram
14. C. Cherlopalli
15. Balamapalli
16. Malugur
17. Nandamurinagar
18. M. Beerapalli
19. Subbireddipalli
20. Kotnur
21. Melapuram-A
22. Melapuram-B
23. Melapuram-C
24. R.T.C. Colony
25. Prashanth Nagar
26. Thyagaraja Nagar
27. K.W. Colony

RESIDENTIAL CAMPS

It is interesting how a vague idea can be transformed into a concrete project. But only when I was actually in the field, confronted with the several aspects of the complex problem that child labour is, did my programme gradually evolve to take a definite shape. This process of revelation happened in clear-cut steps, each unfolding from the previous one. It began by mobilising the child labourers at different work sites and directing them towards the 'Back to School' programme. Seeing that this was far from being the final answer to the problem, we thought of the idea of bridge course centres to help the children cope with rapid learning and get streamlined. In a short period, they should become a part of government-run hostels and village schools.

With the opening of bridge course centres in 26 villages of Peddavaduguru and 27 villages of Hindupur mandals, I thought that I had found a way to deal with the problem, but this feeling of satisfaction did not last very long. I once happened to visit the bridge course centres in some villages along with a few MRPs. In July 1999, I found that some children, in the age group of 10–14 years, were missing from classes in these centres. Due to my close involvement with the work, I could immediately place the missing children. Subhadra, Suhasini and Ramchander Reddy were not attending classes at the bridge course centre at Dimmagudi village, while Vasanta and Bajaramma were missing from the centre at Kandlaguduru village. The children had either gone back to work or had chosen to play truant and stay away from the centre because of sheer laziness or boredom. This is when I began to feel uneasy about the long-term sustainability of my programme.

Shortly afterwards, while passing through Peddavaduguru, I discovered that Kullayamma, a 12-year old SC girl, was not present at the centre too. This surprised me for Kullayamma had clearly been so highly motivated by the 'Back to School' programme that she refused to return to her village, shedding all inhibitions to stay even in the boys hostel so that she could attend school and study in Class I in which she had been admitted. Concerned with her absence, I sent a word to G. Venkatampalli village, saying that I wished to see her. When she did arrive, I was shocked to see the state the girl was in. She walked slowly towards me, dragging her feet as though the very effort was beyond her. She had dead, expressionless eyes and a face that seemed to have suddenly aged. On being questioned gently, Kullayamma confided in me. Her father had died leaving behind four girls and a young boy. All the girls were illiterate and went to work as labourers early in life. Kullayamma enjoyed a brief respite when she joined the 'Back to School' programme and lived in the hostel. However, one day her uncle brutally beat her mother up and forced the helpless woman to send all the four girls back to the fields to work. The young girl said that she was tired of getting up at the crack of dawn everyday to walk to the distant fields, toil there whole day under the scorching sun and then trudge back late in the evening. It was a pathetic and shocking account of human degradation. I asked Kullayamma what she wanted. Looking at me with a pitiable expression, the child replied spontaneously, 'A stomach full of food and a pair of clothes.' I felt a deep sense of pain at this expression of the child's desire, so basic and so small!

Kullayamma's words kept coming back to me and I returned home disturbed and pondered long on what I could do for child labourers like Kullayamma, Subhadra, Suhasini and Ramchander Reddy. I understood that their cases were not isolated or exceptional and that their stories were a living reality of thousands of other children in the area. I felt, the best possible solution, perhaps, would be to have residential camps opened for such children. Being in a healthy, pleasant and hygienic environment all day, where all their needs would be taken care of, without having to face harsh conditions or tussle with conflicting thoughts of earning a few rupees to keep body and soul together, the children would settle down and thrive. Besides, if the fast learning method were to be adopted to eliminate the fear of appearing foolish amongst younger children, as would happen in regular schools, such children would truly enjoy and value the education they received. I felt helpless, however, for I had no staff and the project was operating with meagre funds that would just suffice to keep the bridge course centres in operation. The idea of opening residential camps, attractive as it was, seemed to be an impossible dream. At this juncture, I found myself slipping into a state of depression, and with my project coordinator away on leave, I toyed with the idea of quitting the project.

Thus, it was in a state of turmoil that we went one day to Prashanti Nilayam to meet Sri Satya Sai Baba. Soon two people approached me with the offer of constructing a building. Baba had asked them to do so and it was a timely and useful help.

Realising that the construction of a new building would take a long time, I suggested that we identify old, deserted structures in the village and restore them. After four hours of search, we identified eight sheds of the Schedule Caste Corporation lying unused for more than 10 years.

Baba's people started work on the sheds the very next day and soon converted them into large beautiful classrooms, a kitchen and a storeroom with new bathrooms and toilets. Residential camps for the child labourers were ready.

During this time I happened to meet Vaish, Project Officer, UNICEF. When I spoke about my plans and difficulties, he gave me a piece of paper with the number 2 written and asked me to make a big number. I produced $2 \times 2 \times 2 \times 2$. I was doing something, which was not satisfactory. When I was asked to try again, I thought of 22×22. Vaish prodded me on, and I came up with 22^{22}, but he simply smiled and wrote 2^{222}. I failed to understand why Vaish was keen on making me do mathematics when all I wanted from him was advice regarding my project.

Vaish unveiled the mystery by saying that the point of the exercise was that the scope of a project undertaken could very well be magnified to any extent with sufficient managerial skills. Suddenly, I was clear about what I had to do. By drawing from various sources, I could think of the project taking on bigger dimensions. I immediately started tapping various sources for funds and from a modest budget of Rs 7.70 lakh, the finances increased to more than a crore.

I discovered three more unused government buildings and approached the SC Corporation, district administration and the state government for help in repairing these. We designed wall-to-wall blackboards in all classes and extra blackboards in the dormitories so that the children could scribble. Low tables were also made which had a dual purpose, i.e., children could read and write and also keep their trunk boxes underneath. Next, I was concerned about how to meet the food expenses for the residing children and the salaries of the teachers and other staff at our camps. In this regard, the Social Welfare Department, Government of Andhra Pradesh was requested to provide food for the child labourers. Most of them belonged to the Scheduled Castes, and had joined the 'Back to School' programme. The residential camp facilities were mainly for them. It was a situation entirely without any precedent and we were indeed fortunate to get the sanction. Further, learning that the DPEP was opening bridge course centres in the district, I got in touch with them and handed over our bridge course centres to them. Thus, I was able to use the money, previously earmarked for the bridge course centres, to pay the salaries of teachers and other staff, like the cooks, watchmen and ayahs (workers) required for the camps.

In order to mobilise children for the camps, we undertook a door-to-door campaign. We talked to the poor, illiterate villagers about the novel idea of opening camps for their children. A large number of children were taken in from self-help groups consisting of women from the weaker sections (SC/ST/BC) and the population below the poverty line (BPL). Realising that the incidence of child labour was extremely high among these groups, we addressed the women and spoke to them about the facilities that would be provided to the children in the camps. It was also explained how the children who had missed out on education would not only be helped to go through a fast pace of learning but that their require-ments of uniforms, nutrition as well as overall development would also be taken care of. The response we received was wonderful. The women were only too delighted at the thought that their children would not be illiterate like them. In fact, in many homes, women argued with their men folk and took the final decision in bringing the children for admission in our camps. It was 'women's empowerment' at its best.

The first camp at Peddavaduguru was inaugurated on 14 November 1999 by Kullayamma, who had come to join the camp along with her three illiterate child labourer sisters. A remarkable transformation had come over this girl. Once again, she was a happy child. It was a moment of great satisfaction and joy because I witnessed all grown-up child labourers who had dropped out after 'Back to School' programme troop back into the residential camp[2] with a sense of eagerness and resolution. Residential camps did change many lives, one such change was in Kulla-yamma's life who is now a part of our residential camp.

Kullayamma says,

Destiny willed it that I was born in a poor family. I have one elder and two younger sisters. My father died when I was six years old. He became ill due to excessive drinking, we even had to sell three acres of our land for his treat-ment. At that time, my mother was pregnant and was to deliver soon. We had absolutely nobody to turn to. After my mother delivered, the responsibility of earning came on me and my elder sister. Both of us had to struggle hard, travel to far off places in search of food and at the end of the day we somehow managed to earn Rs 20. We had to go on working till my mother recovered from her delivery. Those were really painful days, the only thing that we thought about was food. Even today the word work gives me the shivers. After a few months, the mobilising team approached my mother. She agreed to send us to the 'Back to School' programme. Soon the three of us joined the

---

2. This is preferable for grown-up child labourers as they need intensive coaching in evenings so that they can pass one class in four to six months. Along with education, overall development is also looked after and children feel quite happy as they are provided with food, clothes and other basic amenities.

bridge course at Peddavaduguru and were happily staying there. The people were very caring. One day I was bitten by a mad dog (late in the night) and I was immediately taken to Anantapur for treatment. After a fortnight I returned and was happy to be back. A week ago, my uncle beat my mother and forced her to bring us back home. Anyway all this is past; today, five of us in the family are going to join the residential camp. There is no going back. My mother is also very happy. Amount of Rs 6,000 have been put in my name. Every month I get Rs 60 which is so useful. Thanks to this way of education, my life has changed for the better. Now in June 2001, I have passed Class VII and I am going to join the regular government hostel.

CULTURAL ACTIVITIES

In order to sustain the interest of the children in these residential camps, it was decided that the teaching/training would not be made too mechanical and boring. There was a clear need for children to take part in extra-curricular activities such as games, music, drama and other cultural activities. This would bring out their latent talents and hone their skills. This would also invigorate the children and help them regain their lost energy (mental and physical).

Narasimhappa of Nimmalakunta village approached me with puppet kits that he was selling. Narasimhappa and his associates had expertise in

Children at one of the child labour residential camps enjoying an educational puppet show

making leather puppets and in organising puppet shows. We discovered educational stories developed by the 'Rishi Valley Educational Society' for this purpose.

I was satisfied with the theme of the stories and felt they could be depicted through puppet shows. This was not an entirely new concept. It was a regular practice in villages to have puppet shows that were both entertaining as well as educating. Puppet shows were organised in the residential camps and the children took part enthusiastically. The youth group leader, Srinu who had helped us in our programme right from conducting the survey to community mobilisation, was engaged as a physical trainer in our project. He was also trained in the art of puppetry and now holds puppet shows every Sunday at the camps.

EDUCATION

Under the guidance of trained and committed teachers, efforts were made to improve the children's academic input. With intensive training, children could pass one class each in every three to four months. The Mandal Resource Persons regularly checked the academic inputs and the curriculum. This was done in all the three camps of Peddavaduguru, Thumakunta and Dimmagudi. The children of Dimmagudi have already passed four classes in one-and-half year and the girls of Peddavaduguru and Thumakunta have passed three classes in one year.

PHYSICAL TRAINING AND SPORTS

Physical activity is a must for the development of children for it promotes overall growth. In the case of these children, this need becomes all the more necessary as they were earlier burdened with heavy responsibilities. Learning and recreation make a child a complete person. Physical exercise brings forth creativity in the children and helps them to spend their energy in a constructive form. Keeping this in view, children in the residential camps were supplied with tennicoits, throwballs and skipping ropes. Each camp required 20 tennicoits, 4 throwballs and 20 skipping ropes. The cost of a tennicoit is Rs 43, throwball is Rs 100 and skipping rope is Rs 16. In the Peddavaduguru camp, a basketball court has also been made available for the children.

**Children playing at a child labour
residential camp in Anantapur**

One hot summer day we went out for a picnic. We lost our way and
the children were thirsty and hungry. After wandering around in the
wilderness for sometime, we came near the Pennar Cement Factory. We
went inside and requested them if we could rest for sometime and also
have some water to drink. We found hospitable hosts in D. Lakshmikantham, General Manager (Works), and his spouse Bharati who offered
us snacks and tea. In the course of our conversation, D. Lakshmikantham
came to know about my work and offered to help our residential camp.
I mentioned our need for sports material, and he was generous enough
to supply tennicoit rings, basketballs, skipping ropes and small balls worth
Rs 10,000. This assistance solved our problem in the sports arena.

HYGIENE

Most of the children enrolled in the camps came from families, where
both the parents are illiterate. Their main concern is to see that the children
get at least one square meal a day. Thus, habits like brushing, bathing,
oiling the hair and chipping nails are often neglected. Conditions of poverty
are pathetic and at times these children cannot even afford a change of
clothes. They play in unhealthy surroundings and become susceptible to

many infectious diseases. Taking all these into consideration, lot of care was taken to see that the children became aware of health and hygiene. They were taught how to keep themselves clean by washing and bathing regularly and soaps were supplied for this purpose. To prevent lice infections, which are contagious, all children were treated with Medicare.

The children in the camps had dry skin. Their skin did not look very healthy either. Dr Swaraj Laxmi, a naturopath, advised us to try oil massage followed by *ubtan* (in Andhra, people know it as *sunnipindi*). *Ubtan* is a powder made from gram and turmeric and it is supposed to do wonders for the skin. I sent my cook to buy 6 litre of coconut oil and 6 kg of *sunnipindi* from our grocery shop. The shopkeeper was surprised and curious to know why we were taking such a large quantity of coconut oil. When my cook explained to him that we needed it for the child labour camps, he immediately offered to donate 6 litre of coconut oil for the residential camp as it was for a good cause.

I wanted to know how much the consumption of oil would there be, thus I personally supervised the three camps. I was amazed to see the amount of oil the children's skin absorbed—their skin was like the parched earth thirsting for a few drops of water.

In the camps, oil massage and *ubtan* is applied to all the children for the purpose of body building, muscle toning and skin care. Coconut oil is used fortnightly and 1 litre is sufficient for a 100 children. The cost of 1 litre of oil is Rs 75. *Ubtan* is used for bathing as it improves the suppleness of the skin and costs Rs 25 per kg. About 2 kg is required for each centre per month (Table 4.2).

Table 4.2
Budget for 100 Children per Month

Item	Quantity (kg)	Rate per Unit (Rs/kg)	Total (Rs)
Coconut Oil	2	75	150
Ubtan	2	25	50
Total			200

MEDICAL CHECK-UP

Medical check-ups were conducted at regular intervals to ensure the general health and physical fitness of the children. Small ailments were

**A doctor conducting regular medical check-up
at Dimmagudi child labour camp**

treated on the spot. However, serious problems were referred to the Head-
quarters Hospital to prevent further complications. A few cases of serious
ailments like a girl suffering from tuberculosis at Peddavaduguru, a boy
with heart ailment at Dimmagudi and a girl who had a very low haemo-
globin content at Thumakunta, were all treated by experts at the Head-
quarters Hospital, Anantapur. Homeopathic pills were distributed to
prevent certain seasonal diseases and other epidemics such as Japanese
Encephalitis, smallpox, etc.

Dr Nagaraju of Peddavaduguru mandal is a dedicated doctor and of
immense help. He regularly conducts check-ups for the camp children.

Child labourers in Anantapur

Before   **After**

Dr Narayanamurthy of Hyderabad organised a free dental check-up for all the child labourers. He persuaded several young dentists from Bangalore to visit the residential camps and he personally supervised the work.

NUTRITIOUS FOOD

Some issues caused serious concern. One of which was the issue of nutrition and health of our children. Most of the children who constitute the labour force in Anantapur district come from poverty-stricken homes. The parents, who struggle for a living, face extreme hardships caused by droughts year after year. Kalpana Sharma in her booklet 'Memories of Drought in Andhra Pradesh' gives Lakshmanamma's version:

> Lakshmanamma ... described vividly the food choices before women: 'When there's no work, there's no money and there's no food. In the afternoon, if there's no food, we have to send the children back to school without any food. We women eat leftovers, usually *kanji*, twice a day. If there is no food, I just lick a little bit of chili powder, drink water and go.'
>
> What are the long-term nutritional and health consequences for these women and the children? The planners know, plenty of studies have established this. But the 'cure' for this disease, which is to give people sustainable livelihoods, has not been addressed.[3]

They can hardly be expected to provide anything close to a balanced meal for their children. In fact, it is this urgent need for food as well as money that drives the young ones to toil hard, crippling their physical and mental development. I was, therefore, determined to ensure that the children in the camps were given healthy as well as tasty food that would not only provide them the necessary nutrition but would also tempt them to stay on with us. Further, it was imperative that the chosen diet be cost-effective in order to be viable.

I learnt about the nutritional value of ragi at a seminar on 'diet and nutrition'. Dr Swaraj Lakshmi of Jindal Institute of Naturopathy at Bangalore helped me in selecting a variety of food items including ragi for the camps. The result was a diet that was affordable, of high nutritional content and suited the taste buds of the young children.

---

3. Sharma, Kalpana, 2000, 'Memories of Drought in Andhra Pradesh'. Hyderabad: UNICEF.

The inmates of the camps were provided a simple and healthy diet mainly in the form of ragi malt and a variety of dishes prepared from sprouted grams that entirely satisfy the body's protein requirements. Besides being easily available in the area, as it is grown here, ragi is also rich in calcium and iodine. It a filling food item which means that the children do not feel hungry for several hours and can concentrate better on their studies as well as other physical activities. This cereal is found to be most effective as a source of instant energy when mixed with jaggery, which also has a high iron content. This kind of a meal is not only nutrition packed but also highly economical and hence an alternative to milk in the diet programme of the children. Jaggery costs as little as Rs 14 per kg and ragi a mere Rs 7 per kg. The cost of sprouted grams is not more than Rs 28 per kg.

1. **Ragi Malt**

Ragi requirement for a day	—	1 kg
Jaggery requirement for a day	—	2.5 kg
Total cost for 15 days	—	Rs 750

2. **Pesalu—Guggillu**
   (Sprouted green grams salad)

Green gram requirement per day	—	1.5 kg
Cost of gram for 15 days would be	—	Rs 675

This means that about a 100 children can be provided nutritious food in the form of a snack for a month at an approximate cost of Rs 1,425. This is an amazing small amount considering the enormity of nutrition value it provides.

Meanwhile, care was taken to observe the effect of the new diet pattern. The results were found to be very encouraging. For instance, it was seen that a girl at the camp who suffered from acute anaemia recovered completely in five months with a daily diet that consisted of an egg, ragi malt and pesalu. The improvement in the general health of the children was clearly evident.

VOCATIONALISATION

No worthwhile human endeavour is known to be completely free of all trials and tribulations. Any venture that is undertaken is bound to face obstacles. It is rightly said that success is sweetest when achieved in the face of overwhelming odds. The same was the case with our residential camps at Anantapur.

About three months after the camps were opened and started progressing satisfactorily with the help of the various programmes meant for rehabilitation of the child labour, suddenly a serious setback occurred in the process of implementation. Vested interests in the form of labour contractors and landlords, who perceived that our project stood in the way of their employing children as cheap labour, instigated the poor parents to pull out their children from the camps. It was easy to persuade the helpless parents to do so by simply threatening to stop doling out the pittance given in the name of financial assistance. Furthermore, a depressing picture was painted of the bleak, hopeless days ahead if the children were to stop working in the fields and quarries and chose instead to study in our camps. This was enough to strike terror in the hearts of the ignorant villagers and many of them took their children out of the camps, which in turn led to a sharp dropout rate. Caught unawares, I was taken aback by the sudden turn of events and the complacency that had begun to envelop me.

I spent days and nights wondering how we could resolve the crisis and entice the children back to our camps. One day, while reading Myron Weiner's book *The Child and the State in India*,[4] I came across a few lines that caught my attention and set me thinking. The moment I read the lines, I knew that I had found a solution to my problem. This book speaks about Gandhiji's views which were subsequently endorsed by the nationalist movement in the Zakir Hussain Committee Report on 'Basic Education'. The Report spoke about how education should be imparted through some craft or productive work. Gandhiji believed that schools could be made self-supporting by imparting education through a productive craft.[5] I was inspired by the idea of associating craft or vocational skills with the children in our camps. Such training could become the core of academic instructions. It could not only educate the children but enable them to become self-sufficient. There was no doubt in my mind that the idea of 'earn while you learn' would greatly appeal to the parents who could be easily convinced into enrolling their children in our child labour camps.

---

4. Weiner, Myron, 1991, *The Child and the State in India*. New Delhi: Oxford University Press.
5. Quoted in Weiner, *The Child and the State in India*, p. 61.

Embroidered matte cards developed by girls at Peddavaduguru

Children learning the vocational course

Farmers of Anantapur depend on a single crop each year and in the event of a failure, the entire village would have no option but to face starvation. Taking this into consideration, we thought that it would be ideal if the children at the residential camps (besides becoming literate) were to equip themselves with occupational skills that would stand them in good stead during lean periods while also enabling them to earn a regular livelihood. I was convinced that such an achievement on the part of our camps would indeed, by itself, be a mark of true success. A meeting with all the teachers and volunteers was convened and the concept was explained in detail. Everybody agreed that if the children are taught some craft or skill that would be a source of income to them, while studying at our camps, their guardians would be more willing to encourage them.

During the initial stage, while preparing a plan of action to vocationalise the education of children in our camps, I happened to meet Sonia Bedi of Young India Project (YIP), a non-governmental organisation involved in social service. In the course of our conversation, I told her about my plans for vocationalisation. She informed me that their organisation was also engaged in training rural women groups in several vocations. One such was the creation of matte embroidered cards which were quite popular. I visited YIP at the first opportunity I got and requested Sonia to extend a helping hand and train some of the child labourers. She agreed and all the girls were trained in this vocation. Some even mastered the skill and were able to produce beautiful cards. It was fulfilling to see the children coming back to the camps. We knew that we had triumphed when a 13-year old Scheduled Caste girl Pedda Gangamma, who was shortly to be married, was admitted to one of the camps by her parents. They were convinced of the success of the vocational programme.

**Children practising 'dip-pot painting'
at a child labour residential camp**

The next craft that was introduced to the children was 'dip pot painting'. I had picked up the skill a few years ago. Dip pot painting is simple to practice as well as to learn. Paints of various hues, a bucket full of water and earthen pot is all that is required. Different colours are sprinkled on the water creating beautiful layers of varied shades on its surface. Then the pot is gently dipped into the water and taken out. The pot gets dyed in rainbow colours and the effect is simply stunning. The children clearly enjoyed the activity and created a variety of beautiful multicoloured pots.

C.C. Venkata Ramudu, MLA, Hindupur, was fascinated by the art of dip painting and spent time along with the children in order to learn the skill.

**C.C. Venkata Ramudu, MLA, Hindupur,
trying his hand at dip painting**

The children presented the dip pots they had created as mementos to several visiting dignitaries. Prominent among them were His Excellency, Dr C. Rangarajan, Governor of Andhra Pradesh, and Her Excellency Dr V. Rama Devi, Governor of Karnataka. The gifts were joyfully received and advice was offered on how the products could be marketed.

Next, we trained our young residents in vocations such as embroidery and tailoring. The District Rural Development Agency, agreed to arrange 10 sewing machines for our centres.

We also came across 'RUDCET', an agency which helped rural un-emeloyed youth acquire vocational skills. We met the people concerned and they graciously agreed to help. They suggested that they would train our children in screen printing.

His Excellency, Mr C. Rangarajan, Governor of Andhra Pradesh admiring the dip painted pots

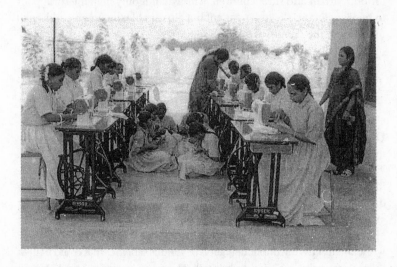

Grown-up child labourers learning tailoring and embroidery at a residential camp

inspiring quotations printed on them. With this objective in mind, I approached a friend's husband, who readily agreed to supply recycled (khadi) paper, which the children could use to make greeting cards. One sheet of paper that could be used to make 15 cards was to cost just Rs 12. Meaningful quotations were gathered from different sources to be printed on the cards by children trained in the skill. Given below are some of the quotations that were used:

- Success is that old A B C ... Ability, Brawn and Courage.
- We must never give up. We must keep on trying even though the times are trying.
- Obstacles are not stopping-stones. They are stepping-stones.

At the back of the card '"Earning while learning" through vocational training' was printed as proposed by Mahatma Gandhi in his scheme on basic education. It was indeed a moment of happiness for each one of us involved with the project as well as for the children themselves. Our products made in the camps were being sold successfully. The parents were content to have their children earn even as little as Rs 10 in the process of becoming literate and acquiring a skill too.

The government can consider the introduction of vocational courses for both urban and rural children. This will not only help the rural poor to become financially independent but also enable the urban children to understand the dignity of labour.

Experiment with Physically Handicapped Child Labour

During my interaction with the villagers, I found a high rate of disability in the Anantapur district. Many disabilities are acquired in childhood. These can be prevented, but lack of awareness and proper medical facilities in villages are responsible for the large number of handicaps. With the help of the Rural Development Trust (an NGO), we formed 21 social groups in 21 villages. Each group consists of people in a village who have either some physical, orthopaedic or visual disability. They meet every week and discuss the implementation of various schemes that could benefit them. Gradually, we tried to bring these groups closer to other women groups. In most cases, disability emerges during the crucial period of 0 to 18 months and it adversely affects the overall development of the child—physical, mental, social, emotional and psychological.

I attended the meetings of the disabled groups and found that there was a lot of bitterness among them. They felt that they were a burden on family and society. When residential camps for child labourers were inaugurated, a few physically handicapped children came to me. I realised that these physically handicapped children were child labourers in the domestic area. On an experimental basis, I decided to keep six physically handicapped child labourers in the camps. The idea was to the break the barriers that they faced with regard to information, education, acquisition of skills, employment and income generation. We also arranged cycles for them.

The children developed affection for us, and their parents were happy that not only were their children being educated but were also learning vocational skills. The government and the community have a collective responsibility for the upliftment of these disabled children. They should work together to provide good residential facilities for handicapped poor children.

Suvarna, a physically handicapped orphan talks about her life in Peddavaduguru Child Labour Residential Camp.

**A physically handicapped girl at one of
the child labour residential camp**

I am a 14-year old girl belonging to the Madiga caste (SC). I am from the Miduthuru village of Peddavaduguru mandal. My mother died a few years back. I have five sisters and two brothers. We are all agricultural workers. I used to attend to domestic work and had never been to school. At times I felt dejected when I saw other children attending school. One day my father heard about the residential child labour camp. He decided to take me there. At first the authorities seemed reluctant and I got nervous and tearful. However, my prayers were answered and I was admitted into the camp. Today I am very happy, my teachers look after me well. I have received so many things here ... they have also given me a cycle. We not only gain knowledge in these camps but also learn about hygiene and discipline. We are provided with good food and also taught vocational skills. I will soon be appearing for S3 stage (Open School System) which is equivalent to Class 6. I hope to complete my graduation. My life has changed, thanks to this residential camp.

Sivamma, an orphan child labourer from Peddavaduguru Child Labour Residential Camp says,

I am from the village of Veerannapalli in Peddavaduguru mandal. I am a 10-year old girl from SC (Madiga) caste. My sister (Nagaveni) and I were brought up by my grandmother. Both of us used to work in the cotton and groundnut fields and also did other works for a living. My grandmother is 60 years old, thus a major burden of earning was on us. Our parents died when we were very young. We were always afraid of what would happen to us after grandmother died. Often, my sister (nine years old) and I would weep in misery. One day we came to know about this residential camp. Today both of us are very happy. Even laughter comes to us naturally. My sister is so much happier, I too feel secure now. School is not monotonous, there are lot of songs and dances. The principal and teachers are really very caring. We both want to study hard and hope to become teachers in the future.

Dileep (10 years/orphan), child labourer at Dimmagudi Child Labour Residential Camp says,

I am from the Peddavaduguru mandal and belong to Mala (SC) caste. When my father died I had to bear the responsibility of earning for the family. We are six brothers and sisters. During the day I had to work and in the evenings I had to take care of my younger siblings. Initially I had to discontinue my studies due to my father's unexpected death. At that point I had studied up to Class I only. Soon my mother admitted me into the child labour residential camp of Dimmagudi. It is now more than two years since I am here. Today I am in the Class VII. I would like to study further.

Kullayappa a resident of the Rauludiki village in Peddavaduguru mandal conveyed his feelings:

> These residential camps are like a boon for our mandal. Initially our children were illiterate and had to work in harsh conditions. It was difficult to stop children from working but today most of them have been admitted into this camp. Parents are also very happy and realise the importance of education. Spacious buildings with a lot of greenery have added 'colour' to our mandal. We are happy that so many deprived children are not only being educated but are also learning vocational skills. The principal and teachers are extremely helpful and take good care of all the children. I truly feel that we are lucky to have two child labour residential camps in our mandal.

Figure 4.1
Graphic Presentation of Child Labourers of Dimmagudi Residential Centre on Their Reasons for not Studying

Dropout

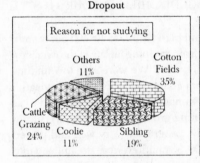

Never Enrolled

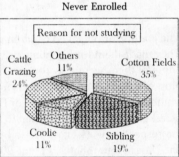

Figure 4.2
Graphic Presentation of Child Labourers of Peddavaduguru Residential Centre on Their Reasons for not Studying

Dropout

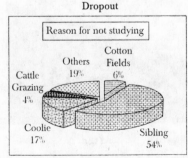

Never Enrolled

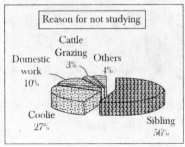

Figure 4.3
*Graphic Presentation of Child Labourers of Thumakunta Residential Centre on
Their Reasons for not Studying*

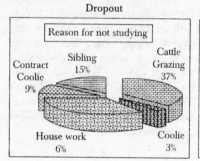

Dropout

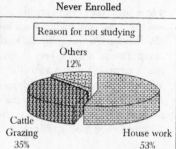

Never Enrolled

DIMMAGUDI CHILD LABOUR HOSTEL

The contractors engaged children and paid Rs 300 to Rs 400 per month.
They made them work continuously from morning till late in the evenings.
Some of them were also contract labourers. We were able to withdraw
most of the older child labourers from cotton fields. For the Dimmagudi
residential camp, the Principal of Dimmagudi High School helped us as
he asked all his school children to bring grown-up child labourers from
the respective work sites. These boys progressed very well and passed
one class in four months. In June 2000, 33 children were streamlined into
government schools and hostels and in June 2001, 29 were streamlined
(Table 4.3).

Before

After

Table 4.3
Break-up of 29 Children Streamlined in Government School and Hostels from Dimmagudi Residential Camp

VII	VIII	Total
11	18	29

Child labourers

Before **After**

PEDDAVADUGURU GIRL CHILD LABOUR CAMP

At Peddavaduguru, a study of the hostel record was conducted in both cases of children, those who have never enrolled as well as those who had dropped out. About 54–56 per cent of children stayed home to take care of their siblings and engage in seasonal agricultural work. The adults migrated from Peddavaduguru to other nearby villages in search of work. They left the older children to look after their siblings. Most of the girls

Before **After**

here looked after their younger siblings and also attended to seasonal agricultural works, such as groundnut, cotton and chilli picking, though work was not available throughout the year.

In this area, schools were found to have just a couple of rooms. There were insufficient number of teachers too. The Peddavaduguru mandal is one of the most backward mandal and here most of the child labourers come from the SC and BC community. After the setting up of the camp, these children have passed three classes each in one year. In all, some 40 students have been streamlined in June 2000 and 52 in June 2001 (Table 4.4).

Table 4.4
Break-up of 52 Children Streamlined in Government School and Hostels from Peddavaduguru Residential Camp

VII	VIII	Total
35	17	52

**Child Labourers after Peddavaduguru
Girl Child Labour Camp Was Built**

Before

After

THUMAKUNTA GIRL CHILD LABOUR CAMP

Thumakunta presents to us an entirely different picture. The major reason for the dropouts and the never enrolled children is domestic work (53 per cent in the never enrolled category and 36 per cent in the case of dropouts). The second major factor is cattle grazing with 35–37 per cent of children engaged in it. The rest are engaged in taking care of the

Before   **After**

siblings and going for coolie and contract work. Silk weaving is the main occupation of people in this area. As one requires expertise in this field, adults are engaged in the work and children are compelled to do the domestic chores. This has contributed to the illiteracy and neglect of these children. There are 100 girls in the training camp and they have passed three classes in one year. The centre's building was renovated by Sri Satya Sai Baba and is one of the most beautiful child labour residential camps. In June 2001, 22 girls were streamlined in Class VIII (Table 4.5).

Table 4.5
Children Streamlined in Government School and Hostels from Thumakunta Residential Camp

VIII	Total
22	22

IMPACT OF THE CHILD LABOUR RESIDENTIAL CAMPS

1. Though initially we had to struggle to withdraw children from work sites and also personally request their parents to admit their children in the child labour residential camps, today after seeing the healthy and nurturing environment of the child labour residential camps, parents themselves are withdrawing their children from works and enrolling them here. In fact sometimes, the number who seek admittance are much more than the capacity.
2. The community is also so sensitised that one person from Parigi has donated his building for starting one more child labour residential camp.

3. Awareness towards 'Right to Education' is clearly visible. In Lepakshi mandal of Anantapur district, a 14-year child labour lost his arm and finally succumbed to the injury. After his death, all the child labourers of Lepakshi wrote a letter to the Collector requesting him to open a child labour residential camp as opened by us (*Vaartha*, 30 March 2001).
4. Four girls have passed the Andhra Pradesh Residential Exam and this speaks about the dedication put in by the principal and teaching staff in the camps. Those who were child labourers till one and a half year back have secured marks at state level. These four girls, till they pass Standard 12 are ensured not only educational facilities but also good residential facilities and extra coaching.
5. Telugu newspapers, like *Eenadu*, *Vaartha* and *Andhra Bhoomi*, and English newspapers, like *The Hindu* and *Deccan Chronicle* are creating awareness about elimination of child labour by writing positive articles about the upkeep of these children, and in a backward place like Anantapur, these camps are treated as oasis in a desert.
6. In these two mandals (i.e., Peddavaduguru and Dimmagudi), teachers and community are fully sensitised and they are owning up this project. This positive gradual change has come and NGOs are also taking up the projects for eradication of child labour.

ANGANWADIS-CUM-CRECHES

During my visits to Peddavaduguru mandal, I came across many girl child labourers especially in the villages of Bheemunipalli, Appecherla and Kristipadu. This made me to look into the social causes that lead to the increase of the dropout rate of girls from schools. Many social practices in our country are discriminatory in nature and have over the years become embedded in the family system. For instance, the oppression and neglect of the girl child has now become accepted in most of the families. Male children are often given more importance because it is assumed that they will bring in income for their family. It is another matter that women are in fact the major contributors to domestic and agricultural sector in the rural area. In many cases, girls are denounced as a 'curse' because huge dowries have to be spent in order to get them married. They are forced to get married at a very early age so that their maternal houses do not have to incur any further expenditure on them. The newspaper is replete with instances of young girls getting married at a very early age. In rural areas, normally marriages take place between 12–14 years. For instance, the Telugu daily newspaper *Eenadu* (19 August 2000) reported the marriage of a 65-year old man to a 14-year old girl (at Rayadurg village in Anantapur district) so that he could have a male progency. This was despite the fact that he had several children, albeit all daughters.

Child marriages lead to a vicious cycle of frequent conceptions, which in turn result in ill health and further degeneration of the woman's physique and psyche. An article in *The Week* (1 October 2000) throws light on child marriages in Maharashtra. Collector of Solapur district of Maharashtra, Deepak Kapoor rightly pointed out in one of the discussions that 'child marriage is one of the reasons for the failure of Family Planning Programmes (FPP)'. The concept of family planning is unknown to many uneducated rural women. However, with the government's drive for FPP, more women are being made aware of these programmes. Although vasectomy is an easier and less complicated operation, it is the women who are often forced to undergo tubectomy. Lack of adequately equipped primary health care centres and the fact that men have the decision-making power makes the situation of women even more difficult.

The Role of the Oldest Girl Child in Rural Families

Girls become mothers when they are barely out of their teens. Before the girl can understand the concept of family planning, she has already borne 4–6 children. Offsprings from child marriages are weak and lack proper nutrition. Neither the mother nor the baby is healthy. In many cases, the eldest girl child has to take the burden of her siblings. She takes on the role of a 'surrogate mother' while the mother is busy with other work in the house or outside. This is the very reason that the eldest daughter is forced to leave school. She is deprived of her right to education. When siblings grow up, it is too late by then to start from where she had left off. Her situation in school becomes awkward. She finds it difficult to adjust to school because she is older than her classmates. She drops out from school and is subsequently made to work so that her income can contribute to the family. This becomes one of the major reasons for her turning into a child labourer.

In a survey conducted in 20 villages of the Peddavaduguru mandal of Anantapur district, it was found that 50 per cent of the female children became child labourers due to this reason. Male children, however, do not have the same reasons for becoming child labourers. In the mandal,

Figure 4.4
Reasons for the Dropout of Girl Children from Peddavaduguru

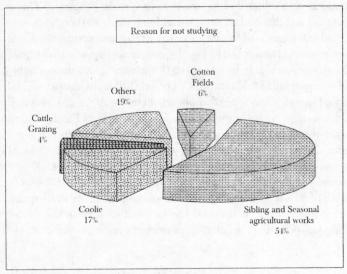

Reason for not studying

Cotton Fields 6%

Others 19%

Cattle Grazing 4%

Coolie 17%

Sibling and Seasonal agricultural works 54%

383 boys and 520 girls were found to be child labourers. These numbers speak for themselves.

In another survey done with 100 girls present in the child labour residential camps, more than 50 per cent of the girls were unable to continue their education. This was because they had to take care of their siblings and also attend to seasonal agricultural work. Figure 4.4 illustrates the reasons for the dropout of these girl children from the schools.

EXISTING INFRASTRUCTURE

In a situation of this kind, anganwadis seem to be one way of bringing back the older girls into the educational mainstream. To put it very simply, anganwadis are pre-schools. They take care of children between the age of 3 and 5. The most important factor is that anganwadis thereby relieve the eldest girl child of the family of her responsibility of looking after these children. Anganwadis are enlarged versions of the urban kindergarten classes which provide elementary knowledge to rural children. Thus, while the younger children go to the anganwadis, the older ones can continue their education at the senior levels. Another advantage of an anganwadi is that it provides good support to the working mothers who no longer need to worry about their children during working hours. Ideally the timings of anganwadis should match those of a regular school whereby all the children are taken care of.

SHORTCOMINGS

When a survey of anganwadis in 36 villages of Anantapur district was conducted, some shortcomings were observed:

1. Anganwadis would close at 12 p.m. in the afternoon while the schools closed at 3.15 p.m. (this forced many older girls to dropout of school in order to take care of siblings).
2. There were no facilities provided for children below three years.
3. Many anganwadis lacked supervision and were built at a distance from the school.

SOLUTION: ANGANWADI-CUM-CRECHE

The ideal solution to this problem would be to have a creche attached to the anganwadis, which in turn should be attached to schools. Creches take care of children below the age of three. At the age of three, children can go to anganwadis. This type of facility is urgently required for working mothers who can go to work peacefully without being deprived of the wages they earn which is essential for running their homes.

Thus, the older children can keep an eye on their younger siblings, who are either in the anganwadi or in the creche, without foregoing their own educational requirements. There is an imperative need to look carefully at each village structure and make provisions for the necessary infrastructure. Anganwadis and creches should be attached to the schools so that principals of the school can supervise them also. The timings of these centres should match regular school timings so that older girls can attend school and in between look after siblings.

While working in Anantapur district, I realised that areas pertaining to child welfare had to be taken care of. Many of the villages in this region lacked basic childcare facilities. The mothers and the older girls here suffered tremendously due to the non-availability of anganwadis or creches.

Anganwadis attached to schools were built in Peddavaduguru mandal in the villages of Kandlaguduru, G. Venkatampalli, Lakshumpalli and Kristipadu. In the Hindupur mandal they were built at Melapuram, Kotnoor, RTC Colony, Kollakunta and Thumakunta Check Post. This was possible with the help of money given by Anantapur Members of Parliament from MPLADS.

Anganwadi attached to a school at Kandlaguduru village

These anganwadis came as a real blessing to these villages. They were developed along specific lines and today they are ideal models. They can be successfully replicated in other regions. Results were immediate after the construction of these anganwadis. The enrolment rates went up immediately in schools, particularly in Kristipadu village. It became clear that such facilities could definitely improve the lives of the villagers.

Thus anganwadis cum creche facility attached to school and timings of these centres as per regular school timings are required for elimination of girl child labour to a greater extent.

Chapter 5

The Need for a New Vision: Bringing in Politicians, Bureaucrats and NGOs

Convergence of Various Departments

To achieve cooperation from many areas one has to converge various activities, monitor and sustain them.

Convergence was thus the answer for this programme too. Initially, though a preliminary survey on the problem of child labour was conducted at the village level, later I travelled extensively in the three mandals of Anantapur district—Peddavaduguru, Gandlapenta and Hindupur—analysing the nature and magnitude of the problem before chalking out a detailed action plan. A study of the data collected established beyond any doubt that the task of rehabilitating child labourers would remain unfinished if the children were merely directed to the 'Back to School' programme. A warm, nurturing environment was needed where the children would not only get elementary school education but would also arm themselves with vocational skills. This would in turn help them to earn their livelihood. The risk of them drifting back to the looms and fields was always a possibility. Thus, an urgent need was felt to set up residential camps that would take up the task of rehabilitating all the child labourers belonging to the surrounding villages.

The setting up of the residential camps appeared at first to be far-fetched with the modest UNDP budget of Rs 7.70 lakh. Sri Satya Sai Baba came to my aid and got one old unutilised building renovated in Thumakunta village of Hindupur mandal. It then occurred to me that one could run the project by getting various government departments involved. The government could contribute to the project either in the form of funds allotted for similar projects or by extending its services, expertise as well as other facilities to our benefit. Such a convergence of all government departments would not only serve to minimise the total expenditure but would also yield the desired result. With the idea taking firm root in my mind, there commenced a search for schemes in various departments that could be appropriate for our programme.

In setting up residential camps for the child labourers, my first task was to arrange for buildings to house them. As the construction of new structures for the purpose was simply not feasible, I had to identify unused or deserted buildings in the area and renovate them for our use. I was able to locate four such dilapidated structures. Two belonged to the Schedule Caste Corporation, while one belonged to the canal building department, and the fourth was an unused community hall. These four buildings had been lying vacant for many years. To convert these into residential camps, renovation was necessary. The construction of boundary walls, large dormitories, classrooms and provision of adequate water supply were some of the tasks that needed to be carried out.

We approached the Social Welfare Department, Government of Andhra Pradesh for assistance. Since most of the enrolled children came from poor SC families, they agreed to meet the food expenses in the residential camps on an experimental basis.

Once the first step was taken, help started pouring in from all sides. I was surprised to find labour officials themselves approaching us to find out what services they could render. The MRPs who worked with me in the field got so closely involved with the project that they took it as a personal challenge. The District Medical and Health Officer did us great service by instructing his Junior Medical Officers to visit our residential camps and conduct regular medical check-ups for the children. Help also came in the form of a noble gesture shown by four local MPs who donated Rs 9 lakh from their MPLAD funds. The money was used for the construction of anganwadis and bridge course rooms, and the Department of Women and Child Development largely coordinated this project. The Deputy Conservator of Forests helped us by giving a variety of saplings for the residential camps. These have flourished under the care of the camp children. The barren, desolate places have been replaced by fully grown plants and nurseries have been set up. District Rural Development Agency (DRDA) assisted us in providing vocational training to the children.

Thus, in an unbelievably short span of time, three beautiful residential camps came up. This was only possible because of the cooperation and convergence of various agencies and departments. The buildings were repaired by the housing department, water supply was provided by the Rural Water Supply Scheme, food charges were borne by the social welfare department, greenery was developed with the help of the forest department, women's group participation was provided by the rural development department and children were rescued from their workplaces with the support of the labour department. I personally looked after the salaries of the principals, teachers, cooks, watchmen and helpers together. I was also in charge of the overall planning and coordination.

The approach of convergence can be used to solve the problem of child labour and perhaps other social evils at the district level. Various departments and ministries under the chairmanship of the district collector/ magistrate can help to generate funds and extend essential services while the salary component can be taken care of by agencies such as the UNICEF, the World Bank and the UNDP.

Possible goals and hard work are a guiding force by themselves. I realised this when, in the midst of my efforts to get various government departments to cooperate and take active interest in the running of our project, I came across a book entitled *Child Labour in India* by Dr Lakshmidhar Mishra, Ex-Secretary, Ministry of Labour, Government of India. I was surprised to discover that Dr Mishra also strongly advocated the convergence of various government departments in tackling the problem of child labour.

The elimination of child labour cannot be the responsibility of a single ministry, department, or agency. A number of ministries, departments and agencies need to come together to pool their energies and resources as will make possible the adoption of a multipronged, convergent, and holistic approach to this complex issue. Those whose involvement is vital to the success of any effort in the context of elimination of child labour are:[1]

As Suggested by Dr Lakshmidhar Mishra		In Anantapur Project
❖ Deptartment of Education	Concerned with UEE, UPE, Operation Blackboard, NFE, DPEP, NLM/TLC.	DEO, APC/DPEP, MEO, MRP's are working.
❖ Deptartment of Women and Child Development	Concerned with implementation of ICDS.	Anganwadis are there and Convergence is brought by UNDP, DPEP and ICDS.
❖ Ministry of Rural Development	Concerned with a number of poverty eradication and rural employment promotion programmes such as IRDP, DWCRA, TRYSEM, DPAP, DDP, JRY, EAS, PMRY.	DWCRA groups (Community mobilisation). Training for income generation to child labour.

1. Mishra, Lakshmidhar, 2000, *Child Labour in India*, p. 7. New Delhi: Oxford University Press. 'In Anantapur Project' is the author's own addition.

❖ Deptartment of Rural Development	Concerned with rural drinking water, rural sanitation, land reforms, CAPART.	
❖ Ministry of Health and Family Welfare	Concerned with the management of Primary Health Centres.	PHC doctors are visiting camps.
❖ Ministry of Labour	Concerned with formulation of labour policy and coordination with state governments for stringent and deterrent enforcement of laws concerning the elimination of child labour.	NCLP camps are there. Labour officials are working for elimination of child labour.

Departments that may be roped in to assist are suggested but I would like to add a few more to the list on the basis of my field experience:

❖ Social Welfare/BC/ST	Dietary and cosmetic charges
❖ Housing Corporation	Repairs of buildings
❖ SC Corporation	Handing over SC shed after repair work
❖ Forest	For plantation and also to make nurseries in the child labour camps
❖ RWS	Water supply
❖ University	Conduct studies and suggest ways to improve it

Further, Dr Mishra talks of setting up a committee of officers, under the chairmanship of the District Magistrate in districts having child labour problem, who will periodically review the problem of child labour in the district to supervise the running of the programme designed to eliminate child labour. It was sheer coincidence that I also had formed a similar committee for overall supervision and review of the work being done in Anantapur district.

Dr Mishra was duly informed about our efforts and the success achieved in this area. He wrote back to express his happiness about the work carried out. He agreed that the Collector's office could play a major role in the elimination of child labour as all departments report to him. He also decided to share the success story of our efforts and initiatives with the district collectors all over the country where child labour projects are running and bring it to the notice of the UNDP representative in India.

CONCLUSION

The convergence of various departments led to the success in the programme of child labour elimination in the two mandals of Peddavaduguru and Hindupur. The number of child labourers who were released, rehabilitated and streamlined in hostels and our residential camps was 2,120. The project was carved out under the chairmanship of the Collector/ District Magistrate. As a national consultant, my role was that of a motivator, catalyst and coordinator. The formation of a committee with membership at the district and block/mandal levels along with the role and responsibility of various departments was listed out.

A single individual or a group or one agency alone cannot solve the problem of child labour. It requires a multi-pronged approach and until and unless convergence with various departments and ministries is brought about, the eradication of this social evil will indeed remain a distant dream.

WHOSE RESPONSIBILITY?

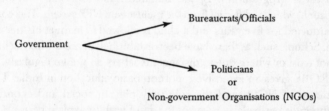

There are many NGOs working in the field of child labour elimination and universalisation of elementary education in India. Some of the renowned and well-known NGOs are Lok Jumbish based in Rajasthan, M.V. Foundation in Andhra Pradesh, Ekalavya in Madhya Pradesh and Creda in Uttar Pradesh.

I had the opportunity to visit two NGOs and study their work in detail. The Mamidipudi Venkatarangaiah (M.V.) Foundation is located in the Ranga Reddy district of Andhra Pradesh. Its main objective is to eliminate child labour. One village activist is assigned to every village and one organiser is provided for every five to seven villages. The foundation has a unique method of funding. Every month a nominal amount on each ration card is collected. The accumulated money (School Development Fund) provides infrastructure, such as school buildings, benches and blackboards for the education of the child labourers in the area. The M.V. Foundation regards all those children who are not part of the school system as child labourers. Teachers associated with this foundation have also created a teachers' union called Bala Karmika Vimochana Vedika which works towards streamlining child labourers into formal schools. M.V. Foundation does not encourage Non Formal Education (NFE). Residential camps are organised for the child labourers. M.V. Foundation also takes the responsibility of teaching in government schools where teachers are fewer in number.

Headed by Anil Bordia, retired Secretary to the Government of India in the Ministry of Education, Lok Jumbish (LJ) is another reputed NGO based in Rajasthan, and its motto is to universalise elementary education. LJ also encourages peoples' participation and works towards the empowerment of women through education. It conducts benchmark surveys and school mapping in order to analyse various educational factors. School mapping involves community participation and thus helps in mobilising people for education. I had the opportunity to visit many villages where the LJ programmes were underway, such as Kedla, Asnawar, Badimanpura and Baria Govardhanapura. SIDA, central and state governments fund these programmes. LJ has initiated Sahej Shiksha (non-formal education) which is different from the mainstream NFE system. This course is conducted for five years and a child is allowed to learn at his/her own pace. Schools such as these have been established in areas where schools do not exist or where due to distances teachers do not go regularly.

PROBE gives an extensive report on basic education in India. Their definition of NGOs and the role they play in social and economic upliftment is particularly relevant to what I wish to explain here.

The report states:

> Non-Government Organisations: Another form of abdication is to expect non-government organisations to supply the missing school facilities. There are many inspiring examples of NGOs' involvement in elementary education. There is also much scope for partnership between NGOs and the state in this field. To expect NGOs to substitute for the government, however, is wishful thinking. Their resources are far too small relative to the needs. Nor is it realistic to expect large public resource could be spent through this channel without disrupting its integrity.[2]

The same report comments: 'It is important to recognise that, as things stand, NGOs actually play a relatively minor role in the education system as a whole.'[3]

---

2. The PROBE Team, 'Public Report on Basic Education in India', p. 137.
3. Ibid., p. 106.

Likewise Dr Lakshmidhar Mishra remarks on the contribution NGOs can make:

> It is evident that the state as an agent of society has failed to provide any protective cover to millions of vulnerable children at their most crucial stage of development. Even though a handful of NGOs have undertaken highly innovative, cost-effective and result oriented initiatives in a few pockets of the country and produced striking results, the fact remains that in terms of coverage or spread this is negligible and uneven.[4]

INITIATIVE TAKEN ON THESE LINES IN THE ANANTAPUR DISTRICT

I was able to use the positive aspects of the NGO's way of working to my advantage as I had enough interaction with M.V. Foundation, Lok Jumbish and few other NGOs. One significant lesson that I learnt was how to commission residential camps. These camps are on-site centres of learning especially set up for the disadvantaged groups. Drawing inspiration from the above we set up residential camps in Anantapur. We focussed not only on education but also on all-round development of children. Our camps covered a wide spectrum right from education, health care, nutrition, hygiene, sports and cultural activities.

Apart from this, the concept of mapping and community participation came from Lok Jumbish. We used a modified model for school mapping and I worked on two other kinds of mapping as explained below:

1. Chart that highlights the school going/educational level of the entire village—School Mapping
2. To study the various reasons that obstruct education especially in below the poverty line (BPL) communities of a particular village—Community Mapping.

On an experimental basis, I was keen to work with the government machinery. I was hopeful that the programme would be successful, and my project coordinator also encouraged me to establish links with government organisations.

---

4. Mishra, Lakshmidhar, 2000, Child Labour in India, p. 321. New Delhi: Oxford University Press.

One of the areas where this was possible was with the DPEP which was functioning in Anantapur. MRPs, who are also teachers, were concentrating on primary education and child labour elimination. Our goals being similar, on my request, we decided to work together. I was particular about bridging the gaps in the DPEP programme. Team work made work easier. MRP Sudhakar Babu from the Peddavaduguru mandal shares his experiences,

> I got involved in this programme along with Narayana Swamy, the mandal literacy organiser. Along with the Consultant, we visited villages to study the problems of child labour and causes for dropouts. I not only gained information in this area but it also became a learning experience. I had the opportunity to visit NGOs like the M.V. Foundation. I also learnt to develop training modules, implement mapping, conduct classes and mobilise the community for this cause. Today, I am proud that we have two residential camps in our mandal. The government has done a great job. We check the educational input, try to streamline these children into regular government hostels and follow up their progress. I am glad we are able to contribute for this noble cause.

This is an example of how government machinery can work with the support of MRPs in the mandal.

THE ROLE OF PEOPLE'S REPRESENTATIVES

The elimination of child labour is not an impossible task. All that is required is appropriate action taken in the right direction by those vested with the power and authority to do so. It is not uncommon to see political leaders give a wide berth to the problem of child labour asserting that it is a direct consequence of poverty, which needs to be tackled first. However, during my project in Anantapur district, politicians also assisted in ways that they could. The role of politicians is important in the area of child labour. People readily respond to authority and this is the reason I wish to emphasise their role. Often it is not the financial constraint that hinders progress but it is the lack of political will or commitment. The case was, however, different in Anantapur district. Several politicians participated in the elimination of child labour. Many of them contributed from their MP funds for the construction of anganwadis, school buildings and other necessary infrastructure. Special mention needs to be made here of C.C. Venkata Ramudu, MLA of the Hindupur mandal who has done excellent work in this area. He was most cooperative and tireless in his efforts to help us build classrooms, and provide infrastructure for our camps. Not only did he participate in the adult literacy camp but also showed keen interest in our vocational programmes. He is keen to have one child labour residential camp in each of his mandals. Drawing inspiration from his activities, his friends also tried to emulate him and provided us with infrastructure for the camps. It was because of his initiative that a few illiterate women became educated with the help of LEADS, a committed NGO at Hyderabad headed by Valli in the field of adult education.

MLA C.C. Venkata Ramudu expressed his opinion,

> This is indeed a unique programme. The idea of convergence is the real force behind the success of this programme. We have been able to contribute to this cause. Many child labourers who are orphans are now educated and in fact have passed three classes in one year. This is a big achievement for my mandal. I believe that with the government's intervention, child labour will no longer be a social evil in my mandal. I hope I can establish two more centres here. Fortunately, I have the support of the community and MRPs.

THE CONTRIBUTION OF THE GOVERNMENT IN THIS AREA

EXISTING SCHEMES FOR CHILD LABOUR ELIMINATION

Two schemes called National Child Labour Project (NCLP) and Non Formal Education (NFE) have been initiated by the central government to tackle the problem of child labour.

Ministry of Labour, on a demonstrative and experimental objective, started the National Child Labour Project (NCLP) in 1988–89 in nine pockets where concentration of child labour is high and it has increased to 100. I visited many districts and observed that this scheme is not running well as funds earmarked for the salaries of the teachers and for feeding the children are inadequate. Ministry of Labour in its manual for the implementation of National Child Labour Projects:

> The scheme of National Child Labour Projects under implementation provides funds for limited number of inputs. These inputs are certainly not exhaustive. District Collector as the Chairperson of the Child Labour Project could improve the content of the programme by complementing the activities under NCLP with that of other programmes in the spirit of convergence.[5]

---

5. Government of India, Policy and Programme for the Rehabilitation of Working Children, p. 63.

This scheme was revised in 1999 and gaps such as regular monitoring and evaluations are emphasised and funds are also increased.

The centrally sponsored scheme of Non Formal Education (NFE) was introduced in 1979–80 on a pilot basis with a view to supporting the formal system in providing education. Implemented in 25 states/union territories, the total coverage of children under NFE is 74 lakh.

PROBE has pointed out that most of these centres are non-functional. Funds flow to the volunteers is highly irregular and meagre. From my personal experience also, I observed that this scheme is for namesake and not fully functional.

Government of India in its publication on Education Guarantee Scheme (EGS) and Alternative and Innovative Education (AIE) (2001: 3) has pointed out:

> The shortcomings of the existing NFE Scheme in terms of very low investments; poor community involvement, problems in release funds; several quality issues including training of instructors, number of hours of teaching per day, etc., had to be addressed.

Keeping the above shortcomings in mind, the Ministry of Human Resource Development and the Department of Elementary Education and Literacy framed the Education Guarantee Scheme (EGS) and Alternative and Innovative Education (AIE) in 2001. These schemes are part of the Sarva Shiksha Abhiyaan (SSA), under which every district prepares a District Elementary Education Plan. EGS has been followed after successful initiative and implementation in the state of Madhya Pradesh. Under EGS and AIE, focus is on the use of community-based micro planning, close linkage with community, quality aspects including the number of hours of teaching, teaching-learning material (TLM), regular academic support through school visits and planning meetings with resource person.

WHOSE RESPONSIBILITY?

GOVERNMENT

Both the governments at the state and national level have to shoulder this responsibility. The state has to take more responsibility in welfare activities. Over the years, the government has gradually shifted responsibility on to the NGOs and private social organisations. A social problem of this magnitude needs immense supervision, wider authority and munificent funds. The government has the necessary infrastructure, enormous manpower and substantial financial resources. The state government should not depend entirely on central government schemes. Ministry of Labour in their Manual on the implementation of NCLP stated:

> It is well known that while Ministry of Labour is concerned with the problem of working children, but there are departments like, Women and Child Development, Education, Rural areas and Employment, Urban Poverty Alleviation, Health and Family Welfare, Welfare, etc. which have separate programmes for promoting well being of children. The magnitude of the problem of child labour being large, there is scope for pooling resources from other sources like the Ministries/Departments indicated above and dovetailing them with the resources available with Ministry of Labour to produce optimal results.[6]

State government can set up a separate department and pool resources from various sources like the UNICEF, World Bank, ILO, private organisations, DPEP and the District Poverty Initiative Programme (DPIP).

POLITICIANS

The role of politicians is equally important in this area. People readily respond to authority and this helps in mobilising community on a larger scale. Anantapur is a classic example of this kind of contribution.

NGOs

I have come to the point I first started with, that no NGO is sufficiently equipped to handle this widespread socio-economic problem. A few NGOs have produced striking results but the fact remains that in terms of coverage or spread this is negligible and uneven. Another problem is that not all NGOs have credibility and one often reads reports about money mismanagement and other malpractices by some of them. Therefore, the government needs to take major responsibility and also inspire reputed NGOs to carry the work forward. For example, when I

---

6. Ibid., p. 63.

withdrew from the programme in April 2000, I enlisted the support of a reputed NGO called the Rural Development Trust. It is run by a Spanish couple, the Ferrers, who have rendered yeomen service in this area for the past 30 years in Anantapur and they are successfully continuing the programme with the help of MRPs (government teachers).

CONCLUSION

Thus, the government (especially the state government) has to create necessary infrastructure network and, if required, enlist the support of reputed NGOs for elimination of child labour. Not to forget the valuable service that can be obtained from politicians.

APPENDIX

It was a pleasure to visit the school and observe the excellent work being done for the girls. I hope you will be able to extend your work to take many more children out of labour and into the educational system.

Good Luck!

Richard H. Young

16 May 2000

UNICEF,
New Delhi

_____

I am very happy. I have visited this place where the dream of Mahatma is being translated into reality.

Rama Devi

5 June 2000

Her Excellency,
Governor of Karnataka

_____

It is a great pleasure to visit this school and see the excellent work that is being done to give education and other forms of training to children who had been employed. Child labour is a social evil which we need to eliminate. I congratulate Mrs Pramila H. Bhargava and all others who have contributed to creating a new home for these children.

Congratulations and wish you all success in your future efforts.

C. Rangarajan

5 June 2000

His Excellency,
Governor of Andhra Pradesh

_____

I visited the Sairaj Government Child Labour Residential School for girls. I have no words to express my admiration for the devotion and commitment shown by the headmaster and the staff to the cause of these children. Though from a disadvantaged background, these children are today bright, sparkling and enthusiastic and looking forward to a future of hope and empowerment.

Lalita Panicker
25 November 2000   *The Times of India*,
New Delhi

My visit to this school has been very rewarding. One gets filled with pride that there are so many well managing committed officers like Mrs Pramila H. Bhargava who are taking special interest in the welfare of these deprived childen. I really congratulate all those who are involved in this very special project and wish them good luck.

K.S. Sarma
23 December 1999   ex-Additional Secretary,
Ministry of Human Resources Development
Government of India,
(At present, CEO, Prasar Bharati)

It is an excellent work done by the UNDP Consultant, the Government Education Department and the Social Welfare Department. The confidence generated among the children is commendable. The dedication of teachers and officials is to be seen to be believed. The project will go a long way to make some of the neglected, destitute and poor good citizens of the nation.

I wish the project full success. God bless all these children. May he give strength to the Consultant to continue this project and extend it to other places also.

S.L. Mital
17 March 2000   ex-Director,
Ministry of Railways
(At present, AGM, IRCON)

The school has good hygienic conditions. The poorest of the poor students have been admitted and the staff is personally concentrating on them as if they were their own children. This real humanity in the school should flourish day by day. We wish that the school becomes a model school.

C.C. Venkata Ramudu
MLA, Hindupur,
Anantapur

The children's camp is really very good in the sense that the children have so much confidence when they sing, when they talk, and write on the blackboard. I am very impressed by the commitment of the teachers and other staff. The children are lucky to have someone like Ms Pramila H. Bhargava to build a future for them. I will cherish this visit of mine to this centre.

Ms Y. Saraswathi Rao
Vice Chancellor,
Sri Krishna Devaraya University

I am indeed fascinated by the excellent work being done in the child labour centre (Residential) Thumakunta today. The synergy forged among all the government departments with shared goals and the inspirational leadership that is provided are too transparent to be missed. The experiment merits replication. The spirit of unity, courage and hope this project has generated is commendable. This project is a real boon to the school dropouts and children who could not avail of the joy of learning and the joy of childhood. I compliment Mrs Pramila H. Bhargava and her dedicated band of staff for running this institute on user friendly and professional lines. I wish this venture well deserved success.

P.L. Sanjeeva Reddy
19 April 2000 ex-Secretary to Government of India,
Department of Company Affairs, New Delhi
(At present, Director, IIPA)

Certainly here one finds the seeds of a more beautiful India.
FELICITATIONS!!!

Cabs Moreno
UNDP, India

Beautiful songs, beautiful dances,
happy faces, and lots and lots of courage!

Dr Alain Jacqvetun
Monitoring Officer,
SAPAP Regional Office, Nepal

CHAPTER 6

CONCLUSION AND PRACTICAL SOLUTIONS

In conclusion, I will briefly discuss the overriding issues, the path taken to establish three of the finest institutions for child labour elemination and discovering some answers to the menace of child labour.

Myron Weiner has pointed out:

> In India no major groups within or outside the government are concerned with enforcing child-labour laws or making education compulsory, for no particular group is moved by theological, ideological, moral, or even self-interest considerations. The result is that officials who prepare central and state budgets merely make incremental changes in yearly educational budgets, officials in state education and labour ministries show no interest in tightening legislation, administrators are not inclined to enforce existing laws, state and local governments pay little attention to elementary education, and teachers sit by idly as children drop out of their classes.
>
> Government officials are fully aware of the international embarrassment that comes with having the world's largest population of child labourers and adult illiterates, but they ascribe the failure to achieve universal education as a result of the country's poverty rather than the government's failure.

He has emphasised the urgent need to make primary education compulsory, outlining how this has been achieved in various countries of Europe as well as in the United States of America, Japan, South Korea and Taiwan. Social anthropologist and United Nations Volunteer Neera Burra, in her book *Born to Work* has stated: 'If there is at all a blueprint for tackling the problem of child labour, it is education.'[1] I am in complete agreement with this most valid and practical suggestion because in the long run, literacy is the only solution to the problem of child labour. However, the opportunity that I had while working in the field and my close interaction with the child labourers, villagers, teachers, members of the village education committees and women groups made me ponder on rehabilitative strategies. Therefore, while it is unquestionable that the best way to prevent the evil of child labour from spreading its tentacles any further is by insisting on primary education and strict family norms, we can, in practical

---

1. Burra, Neera, 1995, *Born to Work: Child Labour in India*, p. 256. New Delhi: Oxford University Press.

terms, deal with the problem of the existing child labour in three significant ways. These solutions are indigenous and hence perfectly suited to the conditions prevailing in our country. They are: the setting up of residential camps, bridge course centres and anganwadi-cum-creche facilities.

WORKABLE SOLUTIONS: SOME ANSWERS

It is certain that solutions exist for any problem. There are answers to the questions posed in the preceding section. In this section, we shall consider what these answers could be. I have closely studied, analysed, discussed to come to these conclusions. However, some of the answers/solutions also arose as a response to the survival instinct. Not all of them are applicable at the same time or at the same place. However, one thing is clear; they are based on my experience in the field. Perhaps, the results from these may not be immediate or with the same kind of success, but these solutions are practical and useful.

Following are the practical solutions for the eradication of child labour.

1. Residential child camps for older child labourers.
2. Bridge courses and special classes for child labourers between the age of 6–9.
3. Anganwadi and creche facilities.
4. Necessary infrastructure.
5. Vocational and professional training.
6. Convergence and tapping of all resources.
7. Utilisation of all existing government resources.
8. Community participation.
9. Participation of women's welfare organisations.
10. Strict enforcement of family planning norms (especially for men).
11. Enforcement of labour laws.
12. Motivation.

Let us now look closely at each of these points and see how they can contribute in solving the problem.

RESIDENTIAL CAMPS

Residential camps are a must for older child labourers (9–14 years) as they require a fast-paced system of education. In many cases, they have missed some form of regular schooling. These camps lay emphasis on the overall development of the child, i.e., in the areas of education, health and hygiene, sports and physical activities, and vocational training. Each of these areas should be closely monitored and evaluated periodically.

BRIDGE COURSES

Bridge courses are specifically required for children in the age-group of 6–9 in their own villages. For every 20 children, there should be one bridge course volunteer who will teach them and also pay extra attention to the weak students. These volunteers can be called 'local tutors' or 'tuition masters', who might often have to hold special classes in the evening.

It is a fact that one requires some amount of money for running bridge courses. Where should this money come from? A nominal sum of perhaps Rs 5 can be collected on each ration card towards the 'School Development Fund'. It is not difficult to gather such a small amount and, moreover, it is not always possible to depend on the government or other donor agencies for this contribution. Also, it develops a sense of pride in the villagers when they contribute towards their own welfare.

ANGANWADIS AND CRECHE FACILITIES

In villages, anganwadis along with creche facilities are a must. They must be built adjacent to the regular schools. Furthermore, the working hours of anganwadis and creches must match with those of the regular school, otherwise the purpose is lost.

NECESSARY INFRASTRUCTURE

Space is a matter of primary consideration when plans are made for the functioning of residential camps, bridge course centres, anganwadis and creches. The success of these programmes would depend, to a great extent, on the availability of proper buildings. Very often there are government buildings which are either lying vacant or unused. These can be repaired, renovated and put to use as residential camps.

Bridge course rooms can be acquired from schools, if available, or such rooms can be constructed in schools with money obtained from donors or from MPLADS funds. These basic suggestions can be further applied to the cause of anganwadi and creche facilities also.

Vocational and Professional Training

Blending vocational training with academic learning seems more practical. This is not only because the skill that is acquired will equip the children to earn a living in the future, but also because the marketed products created by the children, in the course of the training, will be an immediate source of income. The children, thereby, learn to believe in the dignity of labour and to appreciate the importance of money. In addition, if the children manage to earn even Rs 10 a day (in the process of learning a useful trade), their parents will no longer send them to toil hard in fields or quarries.

Convergence and Tapping of All Resources

Various departments of the government have to come together, or converge, in order to eliminate the evil of child labour. A united effort is required to create residential camps, anganwadis and creches, which will in turn provide an alternative system of sustenance. This new system can gradually eliminate the need to send children out to work. Convergence has to be carried out under the effective guidance and chairmanship of the district collector/magistrate as he is the head of the district. For example, the convergence established at Anantapur was appreciated by Lakshmi-dhar Mishra, Ex-Secretary, Ministry of Labour. Subsequently, he circulated copies of the convergence documents to all district collectors involved in child labour projects, throughout India.

Departments like housing, education, forestry and rural development can be converged to work together. NGOs by themselves cannot tackle a problem of this magnitude, but if they are supported by all the government departments, it will definitely lead to success and will be a simpler task to achieve.

Acquisition of necessary fund(s) can be done at the state level. The state government has the necessary power and the required machinery to facilitate such a task. Several voluntary agencies have come forward with offers of money to help a good cause. *The Economic Times* (26 September 2000) mentions the efforts of WIPRO in this area.

Azim Premji has long held the view that primary education in India needs lots of funds and encouragement, especially from the private sector.

He recently floated the Azim Premji Charitable Foundation to work in the field of education mainly at the primary level. This is a private initiative of Mr. Premji.

He has transferred 2,68,500 shares to this foundation and has disclaimed beneficial ownership of these shares.

At Monday's price, the shares given to this foundation were worth 76.43 Crores.

Infosys is another example. Also, Sri Satya Sai Baba has done tremendous service in the field of education. Head of a state can tap these resources and direct it to the areas of greatest need (AP has already tapped the Azim Premji funds).

Rural India has witnessed varying forms of development interventions towards poverty alleviation, employment and income generation, sustainable development and so on. However, these schemes have made only a marginal impact on the lives of children, as there is no sign of a major decline in the incidence of child labour. Under convergence, the main aim would be to ensure that the rural development department forcuses on child labour households and facilitates improvement in livelihood resources.

Utilisation of All Existing Government Resources

It is possible to tackle this problem with the existing government machinery. For example, MRPs worked efficiently in the functioning of the residential camps for child labourers in Anantapur district. However, I would also recommend that they be given some special honorarium as an incentive for the extra work they do. They have vital experience in fieldwork and they can focus attention on the specific needs of the locality. They have the required data on school dropouts and the reasons for it. Their familiarity with the community makes them ideal for mobilising and inspiring the people. Unfortunately, MRPs are used more for office work, when they should be ideally working in the field. Even after the DPEP scheme draws to a close, MRPs should be allowed to continue their work. In spite of my withdrawal from the project, MRPs are effectively continuing the work.

TEACHERS

The human element in any endeavour is the most vital feature. If teachers are provided the right atmosphere and have the ability to motivate, half the battle of getting children into schools is won. Teachers themselves need to be resourceful, well-educated and highly motivated. Therefore, teachers who do good work must be honoured and encouraged with awards and certificates of merit. A community that respects teachers will see their children making progress.

COMMUNITY PARTICIPATION

The community should be actively involved in a major way. This is absolutely necessary as they should be ready to take over and monitor the provided facilities when the original group that establishes it withdraws. Women from self-help groups, members of the village education committee and youth groups prove effective in this area of community participation.

The role of the community cannot be undervalued in the eradication of child labour. A village-level committee can be formed which should consist of the principal, sarpanch, Village Administrative Officer, Village Development Officer, youth groups, SHG and DWCRA groups. This committee can monitor several areas, such as the appointment of local tutors, school performance and dropout rate. Communities have to come forward and shoulder this responsibility in the area of raising funds. Funding agencies and foreign donors (such as World Bank, UNICEF and UNDP) will not always be there. Local solutions have to be evolved for local problems.

School education committees should not be present only for namesake but actually function in practice. About 90 per cent of school education committees are non-functional. This is because they are not aware of their roles and responsibilities. On an experimental basis, the local school committee chairmen were called for a meeting in our residential camps and felicitated by us. This public recognition of their work brought about a tremendous change in their attitude towards the community and its members.

YOUTH GROUPS

Youth groups are the perfect vehicles for tackling the problem of child labour. In Hindupur and Peddavaduguru mandals, the Jana Vignana Vedika youth groups contributed greatly towards our work. They enacted plays which helped us in mobilising child labourers for residential camps.

PARTICIPATION OF WOMEN'S WELFARE ORGANISATIONS

Several women welfare organisations, like the Army and Railway Officers' Wives, are involved in welfare activities. Certain states have formed welfare organisations run by these officers' wives, for instance, Aakansha in Uttar Pradesh. Ideally, the district collector/magistrate should initiate such active participatory movements. Groups can work together, but unlike the convergence of government departments, here the stress can be on the convergence of non-formal groups.

STRICT ENFORCEMENT OF FAMILY PLANNING NORMS

One of the root causes underlying many of the problems that India as a country faces is overpopulation. At present, it has touched the one billion mark. Resources and infrastructure remain fixed but the number accessing it grows continuously. This creates numerous problems, be it in the area of basic necessities or better amenities. Thus, relentless growth has to be controlled by means of strict regulations and prohibitions, through family planning measures. Men especially have to be mobilised.

Such measures should be enforced strictly. This will not only lead to a drop in the growth rate of population but will also trigger off a decline in child labour.

ENFORCEMENT OF LABOUR LAWS

There are various articles in the Indian constitution which safeguard the interests of children. These rules and regulations existing under the Indian

Labour Law should be strictly enforced by the labour department. Enforcement of the law is as important as all other prerequisites for child labour elimination. The recent case of Nike cancelling its contract with a Cambodian garment factory because of the latter's use of under-age workers should be noted (*The Economic Times*, 4 October 2000: 12). It is ironical that in India we refuse to act even when the most distressing facts are revealed to us.

MOTIVATION

This is a vital key to the success and implementation of any programme. The personnel working with children in any field have to be totally involved and self-motivated to give them their best. If this personal touch is absent, it becomes difficult. Motivating those involved in such programmes is necessary. Thus, the collector motivates his officers, who in turn motivate the people working under them. This has a magical effect on the entire system. Motivation can be in the form of appreciation, praise or even monetary rewards, but it is absolutely essential and will go a long way in eliminating many of our social evils.

The implementation of similar programmes to deal with the problem of child labour on a much larger scale with a view to completely eliminate it may be undertaken by different states in the country. By selecting a single district or even one mandal or block could be the mark of the beginning of a long term mission. Extensive surveys conducted with the aid of mapping, education registers and other techniques outlined in the workbook can be closely followed by relevant corrective measures. The programme, after achieving success in one mandal, can then be carried forward to other areas in the state marked by similar problems. Besides NGOs, the government can seek the assistance of various private agencies which would be willing to help. Many organisations and business houses in the private sector can be approached in this respect. All such cooperative efforts can be carried out under the chairmanship of the district magistrate/collector, as he is head of all departments.

Finally, some measures that should be immediately taken care of:

1. To address the immediate problems of streamlining child labourers who are already in the age-group of 7–14 years, necessary infrastructure such as bridge courses, residential camps and anganwadis-cum-creches need to be provided and a programme of minimum three years to be pursued

continuously, if total rehabilitation has to be effected. Meanwhile, primary education to be made compulsory and labour laws dealing with child labour to be enforced strictly. Otherwise we will be adding worthless human resource that will be a burden to our country forever.

2. The government needs to include child labour as the 21st point in its programme, in which, at present, 20 points such as defence, education and rural development are taken care of. There is, as a matter of fact, an urgent need to focus on child labour elimination as the most important aspect of the government programme.

3. There is imperative need to open a separate department to deal with the problem of child labour and have funds earmarked for the purpose. The government can opt to operate the 'development fund' for this cause for which donor organisations and foreign agencies will be happy to contribute generously.

4. State government has to take lead and increase share of SDP (State Domestic Product). Private investment can be encouraged. For example, the best performing states like Kerala, Tamil Nadu and Himachal Pradesh have received substantial private investment in education.

I end this book with the faith that in the field of child labour elimination: **'The government can do it.'**

CHAPTER 7

GUIDE FOR NEW ENDEAVOURS:
A PRACTICAL WORKBOOK

This workbook is a guide for those who want to initiate programmes for the elimination of child labour or carry out any research work. It includes survey forms, training modules, costs involved, question forms, mappings, labour laws and monitoring registers. The workbook provides rough guidelines. They can be modified to suit the situation and needs of a particular mandal/block of a district. It is advisable to carry out the programme in one mandal and subsequently replicate it in other mandals. These initiatives can be undertaken by the government or NGOs. Universities can also conduct research.

PROCESS

1. Selection of a district for implementation of the Child Labour Project (CLP). The project can be undertaken under the chairmanship of the Collector/District Magistrate. District-level committee to be formed.

2. Mandal/block-level committee to be formed.

3. Selection of local monitoring team by the mandal core team.

4. Preparation of training module by the mandal core team for conducting door-to-door survey as well as mobilising the community.

5. Conducting training for the community survey. The training sessions will have to attend to the following details:

   (a) Participants.
   (b) Subjects to be covered in the training module.
   (c) Cost.

(*d*) Survey forms:

    (*i*) Forms I and II (Village Education Register)
    (*ii*) Simple forms

6. Consolidation and analysis of data.

    (*a*) Number of small child labourers (6–9 years).
    (*b*) Number of grown-up child labourers (9–14 years).

7. Selection of volunteers to carry out the bridge course. The number of volunteers to be selected will depend on the previous analysis and one bridge course teacher to be appointed for every 20 children.

8. Preparation of bridge course material/Rishi Valley kit/the standard formal books.

9. Training of bridge course teachers. The training session covers the following aspects:

    (*a*) Duration.
    (*b*) Cost of training
    (*c*) Community mapping.
    (*d*) Preparation of registers.

        (*i*) Community registers.
        (*ii*) Monitoring registers.

    (*e*) Emphasis on joyful method of learning.
    (*f*) To act as local tutors.

10. Residential camps.

    (*a*) Convergence.
    (*b*) Selection of principal, teachers and staff.
    (*c*) Training.
    (*d*) Budget.
    (*e*) Evaluation of students.
    (*f*) Evaluation of teachers.
    (*g*) Monitoring registers.
    (*h*) Overall development.
    (*i*) Streamlining.

11. Community mobilisation.

   (*a*) Teacher community.
   (*b*) Women groups.
   (*c*) Youth groups.
   (*d*) Labour officials (labour laws enclosed).
   (*e*) Local police and revenue officials.
   (*f*) Local politicians.

12. Anganwadis and creches.

13. Budget.

14. Process documentation.

   (*a*) SWOT analysis.
   (*b*) Questionnaire for conducting research by universities.

15. Bridge the gaps found in this project.

16. Go for replication in other mandals/blocks.

PROCESS DETAILS

1. Constitution of District Team and Selection of Mandal/Block for Child Labour Elimination Programme

Under the chairmanship of the Collector/District Magistrate, the following core committee can be formed in order to undertake the Child Labour Programme (CLP).

District-level Committee

Chairman: District Collector/Magistrate.
Convener: Any officer appointed by the Collector who will be in charge of the CLP and will report to the Collector.

Members

   (*a*) District Education Officer.

(b) Additional Project Coordinator, District Primary Education Programme (DPEP) (in case DPEP programme is being carried out in the district).
(c) Deputy Director, Adult Education.
(d) Deputy Director, Social Welfare.
(e) Project Director, ICDS.
(f) Project Director, National Child Labour Project.
(g) District Manager, Housing Corporation.
(h) District Forest Officer and Deputy Conservator of Forests.
(i) District Medical and Health Officer.
(j) Project Director, District Rural Development Agency.
(k) Project Officer, Non Formal Education.
(l) Labour Officer.
(m) Reputed NGO.

Selection of a Mandal/Block where Child Labour is High

The district team will decide on a mandal/block where CLP can be implemented. Their decision can be based on the following factors:

(a) The economic backwardness of a region.
(b) High incidence of child labour.
(c) Effective mandal team (Mandal Education Officer and Mandal Resource Persons/teachers).

(Certain figures regarding literacy rate, dropout rate, number of villages in a mandal/block can be collected as given in Annexure 1.1).

2. Mandal/Block-level Committee

Convener: Mandal Education Officer (MEO).

Members

(a) Mandal Revenue Officer (MRO).
(b) Mandal Parishad Development Officer (MPDO).
(c) Mandal Resource Persons–DPEP Scheme (MRP).
(d) Mandal Girl Child Development Officer (MGCDO).
(e) Mandal Literacy Organiser (MLO).
(f) Labour Officer (LO).
(g) Child Development Programme Officer–ICDS.
(h) Doctor, Public Health Centre.
(i) Circle Inspector/Sub-Inspector, Police Department.

The Mandal Resource Persons (MRPs) and Mandal Girl Child Development Officer (MGCDO) are usually associated with DPEP. In case the mandal or block is not covered by DPEP, two or three dedicated and hard working teachers can be nominated for the implementation of CLP.

Budget

The budget required at this level can cover the honorarium to be paid to all the Mandal Resource Persons/nominated teachers at the rate of Rs 1,000 to 1,500 per month per person.

3. Selection of Local Monitoring Team at the Village Level by Mandal Core Team

- 'Local monitoring team' can consist of the school headmaster, school committee chairman, two members from women's groups and two active dedicated youth members. Under the leadership of the headmaster, the group can monitor the performance of bridge course teachers/local tutors.
- 'Local core team' can consist of headmaster, sarpanch, Village Development Officer (VDO), anganwadi workers, Village Administrative Officer (VAO), two women representatives and two members from youth groups. They can meet fortnightly or monthly.

Their task is to monitor overall education aspects of a village and also develop 'School Development Fund' which can be used for:

- Infrastructure.
- Payment to bridge course teacher.
- Any other requirement related to the educational aspect.

4. Preparation of Training Module by the Mandal-level Committee

The training module is meant for conducting door-to-door survey as well as for mobilising the community. The training module should be prepared mainly by MRPs/teachers and can include subjects such as:

(a) What is child labour and the causes for low enrolment and dropouts.
(b) Need for education and providing information about the existing facilities available with the government such as Scheduled Caste/Scheduled Tribe/ Backward Caste hostels, anganwadis, non-formal education set-ups, open schools and the National Child Labour Project (NCLP scheme).

(c) How to conduct surveys and make school mappings.
(d) Role of teachers.
(e) Role and responsibility of the community.
(f) Sensitising the community by showing them video cassettes on child labour.

5. Conducting Training for Door-to-Door Survey and Community Mobilisation

(a) Duration: two days.

(b) Participants: two to three teachers, two persons from youth groups, and one woman (preferably literate) from women's groups and the Chairman of the School Education Committee.

(c) Cost: maximum Rs 40 per participant for food and travel expenses (i.e., TA/DA).

(d) Forms I and II:

    (i) Form I: for individual family.
    Form II: for consolidating information about 10 families. This will form the Village Education Register and it can be maintained for 5 years (Annexures 2.1 and 2.2).

or

    (ii) Simple forms can also be adopted.
    Any form among these can be used as per convenience of the trainers and participants. (Annexures 3.1, 3.2 and 3.3).

(e) School Mapping: Mapping of the selected schools can be done based upon the information given in Forms I and II. The school mapping procedure reflects the various facilities available in a particular village. For example, the mapping can be done in the following manner:

(i)	Boy attending school	: ▲
(ii)	Boy not attending school	: △
(iii)	Girl attending school	: ●
(iv)	Girl not attending school	: ○
(v)	Child attending anganwadi	: ▬
(vi)	Child not attending anganwadi	: ▢
(vii)	A family	: ⬠

The mapping for a particular family may be as follows:

Triangle symbol is for boy and circle is for girl. When they are blank it means their life is blank (no education). A sample is enclosed—one blank form and one filled form in Annexures 4.1 and 4.2—for guidance.

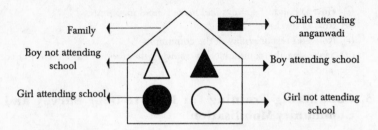

Not only education status but also information about the presence of primary school, upper primary school, anganwadi, post office, dispensary, railway line, mountains, good roads, and also total population (males and females in the particular village) can be charted out in this school mapping.

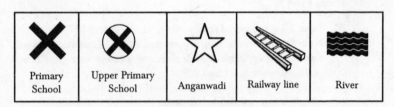

6. Consolidation and Analysis of the Data

Data collected through the surveys can be consolidated for the entire mandal (Annexures 5.1 and 5.2). This consolidated data will give a clear picture about the number of child labourers present in each and every village. For the purpose of consolidation and analysis of the data, every child out of school is considered as a child labourer. Follow-up action requires the categorisation of children into small child labourers (6–9 years) and grown-up child labourers (9–14 years).

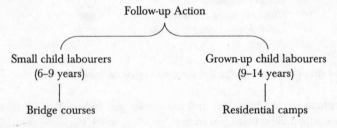

(One blank and one filled up sample forms in Annexures 5.1 and 5.2).

7. Selection of Bridge Course Teachers

Bridge courses are to be provided for child labourers between 6 to 9 years of age in their respective villages. In each village, the bridge course teachers are to be selected in the ratio of 1:20. For example, one bridge course teacher can be selected for every 20 child labourers between the age of 6 and 9. While selecting the bridge course teachers, the following criteria has to be kept in mind:

(a) Selection of the teachers to be done by the mandal core committee in consultation with local monitoring team.

(b) Minimum qualification for the teachers to be decided by the mandal core committee.

(c) Candidates from the same village to be preferred.

(d) Dedicated persons to be selected.

The bridge course teacher's responsibility is to bridge the gap for the dropout/never enrolled child. In other words, the teachers should ensure fast paced learning for the small child labourers so that they can pass two or three classes in one year and can be streamlined into the formal schools. Weak students can join the bridge course too. The teacher has to act as a local tutor as well. Since the parents of most of the child labourers are illiterate and are exhausted after the day's work, they are unable to tutor their children. Therefore, the bridge course teacher should be willing to provide extra coaching for the children in the evenings as well. The headmasters and the community should supervise the work of these teachers.

Budget

They can be paid Rs 1,000 per month. With the cost of escalation, it has to be reviewed in the future.

8. Preparation of Bridge Course Material/Rishi Valley Kit/Standard Formal Textbooks

In our project, we prepared three textbooks, i.e., on mathematics, environmental science and the regional language, i.e., Telugu, with the help of six MRPs (teachers). The emphasis during preparation of this material was on the joyful method of learning as it is important to engage the attention of the child labourers and ensure that they enjoy their lessons.

Simple language and a number of games were included so that the children could enjoy their lessons. We also used the kit developed by the Rishi Valley School for teaching. However, it is optional as to which method should be followed. Standard school textbooks can also be used.

9. Training for Bridge Course/Residential Camp Teachers

(a) Initial training can be given for 10 days. This can be followed up every month with a one day refresher training.

(b) Emphasis to be laid on 'playful/joyful method of learning' (lot of games to be taught).

(c) Community mapping to be taught for the below poverty level groups, so that the correct reason for child labour in a particular village can be traced. (For instance, in Melapuram village, the long distance to school is a reason for children not attending school, while in Thumakunta, it is because of cattle grazing. Two village maps are attached for further guidance in Annexures 6.1, 6.2 and 6.3.)

(d) Teachers to be asked to maintain registers. These registers can be simple and must graphically depict the progress made by a child from one class to another. Reasons for the child becoming a child labourer is depicted through pictures (one sample page of a register is included in Annexures 7.1–7.4).

(e) The bridge course teachers to also act as local tutors and give tuitions to the child labourers in the evening as well. Follow-up work even after the school timings is important as the child labourers have to keep pace with normal school schedules. They have to be sensitised for taking up evening classes.

(f) Bridge course teachers to ensure that these children undergo fast paced learning (to pass one class in 4–6 months till they reach Class III).

(g) Course material (local made or standard books) briefing to be given.

(h) In case community volunteers are present they can maintain community figures, otherwise bridge course volunteers can maintain figures for dropout/never enrolled children (Sample of the register in Annexures 8.1, 8.2 and 8.3).

10. Residential Camps

(a) Convergence

This is very vital for setting up residential camps for grown up child labourers (9–14 years). Following requirements can be taken care of by various departments.

- Education—Supply of books and academic check-up.
- Housing—Old building which is unutilised can be repaired with the help of the housing department.
- Water—Water supply department can supply the water.
- Diet and Cosmetic charges—The responsibility can be given to the nearby SW/BC/ST welfare hostels as they have expertise in handling hostels.
- Health—Check-ups can be done by doctors available at the local level.
- Seeds and Plants—DFO and DCF (Conservator, Forest) can provide seeds and plants.
- Revenue—For giving local support at the mandal/block level.
- Labour and Police—For withdrawing children from hazardous and non-hazardous work sites (Annexure 9.1).

(*b*) Selection of Principal, Teachers and Staff

- Due care is to be given. As dealing with child labourers one has to be fully sensitised and responsible. For every 20 children one teacher can be appointed.

For 100 children	
	■ 1 principal
	■ 5 teachers + 1 vocational teacher
	■ 2 cooks
	■ 1 attender
	■ 1 watchman
	■ 1 sweeper

(*c*) Training

- Initial training to be given for 10 days. Course material briefing and how to maintain registers, monitor progress, joyful method of learning, sensitising principal and teachers towards child labourers' emotional need. Cost of trainees per day maximum Rs 40 and trainer (two numbers) maximum Rs 80 per day.

(*d*) Budget

- One copy of budget to run residential camp is enclosed. However, as per the cost of escalation, it can be modified (Annexure 10.1).

(*e*) Evaluation of Students

- One evaluation sheet is enclosed (Annexure 11.1). As per this, above average (AV), average (A) and below average (BA) grading to be given.

Accordingly special evening classes to be held for average and below average students.
- Preferably Mandal Resource Persons (MRPs)/teachers from outside this campus to check it monthly.

(f) Evaluation of Teachers

- Evaluation of teachers can be done quarterly. To motivate and give recognition, 'best teacher' award can be conferred quarterly. Evaluation not to be done only for education, but also for health, hygiene, sports, cultural activities, maintaining plants, physical activities and overall development of the child labourers enrolled.

(g) Monitoring Registers

- One simple sheet for every child can be maintained in a register. It must tell the case history of a child, pictorial presentation of child dropping out and graphical presentation of child passing out of each class (Annexures 12.1, 12.2 and 12.3).

(h) Overall Development

- Here focus is to be given on overall development of children through education, culture, sports, maintaining hygiene habits, cleanliness of the campus, looking after plants (one child can look after five plants), discipline, respect for elders and vocationalisation (chart enclosed [Annexure 13.1]).

(i) Streamlining

- Totally illiterate children can be made to go through fast paced learning, as they are grown-up and their grasping power is quite good. They can get Class III in one year (one class in four months). Later on six months can be allotted. However, all efforts may be taken to streamline these children into regular hostels and regular schools.
- The purpose of these residential camps is to help grown-up child labourers make up for their lost years and then streamline them into regular formal schooling pattern after acquiring elementary knowledge as well as vocational skills.

11. Community Mobilisation

- To mobilise children for bridge courses and residential camps, it is advised to take help of local people. For example, the headmaster and teachers can be effective.
- Next, women's groups (In A.P., they have formed self-help groups from BPL poor groups and most of the child labourers are found in these groups). These groups are also effective in withdrawing children.
- Contribution of youth groups cannot be underestimated. Youth can play a very effective role.
- Labour officials to withdraw children effectively. (A brief of labour laws related to child labour elimination is in Annexures 14.1–14.8.)
- Police can also help in withdrawing children.
- Local politicians, i.e., MPs and MLAs can contribute significantly.

Precaution: All these efforts given earlier can be implemented effectively only if necessary infrastructure exists to absorb the withdrawn children, i.e., bridge courses in the respective villages and residential camps, for grown-up children. Otherwise, withdrawn child labourers cannot get absorbed and it will turn out to be futile practice.

12. Anganwadis and Creches

- On an experimental basis, a few anganwadis along with creche facilities attached to the school can be made. The timings can correspond with regular school timings. Mothers' committee to be formed for monitoring these anganwadis. One teacher also to be included in this mothers' committee. In some places mothers' committee exists, but it is only for namesake. It has to be activated.
- This will help in girl child labourer to join school who has to forgo school to look after younger siblings. Each anganwadi worker and ayah to be paid extra amount of Rs 300 (approximately) for extension of timings.

13. Budget

(a) It should focus on three main points:

(i) Residential camps (9–14 year old child labourers)
(ii) Bridge courses (7–9 year old child labourers)
(iii) Anganwadi cum creche (0–5 years children)

(*b*) Training.

(*c*) Community mobilisation.

(*d*) One Child Labour Officer (CLO) in each district.

(*e*) One Child Labour Programme Manager (CLPM) at state level.

(*f*) Total budget at the state level for one year (programme to run continuously for 12 months) comes to approximately Rs 295 + 5 crore = Rs 300 crore. (5 crore for one state-level programme manager, 23 district child labour officers, and staff and establishment.) Thus minimum Rs 300 crore are required for a one year continuous child labour eradication programme (Annexure 15.1).

Note: This programme is only possible if district convergence is used and unutilised buildings are repaired by the government and government takes over the maintenance of the buildings.

14. Process Documentation

- After successful implementation of the CLP, SWOT (strength, weakness, opportunities and threat) analysis to be carried out.
- Process documentation from starting of the initiative to the end to be recorded. It should include:

  - Financial implication (budget),
  - Human resource involved,
  - Cost-effectiveness,
  - Material used (forms, mapping, training modules, etc.),
  - Shortcomings, and
  - Achievements

- Universities can also conduct research studies (one questionnaire form enclosed in Annexures 16.1–16.5).

15. Bridge the Gaps Found in this Project

Whatever shortcomings and obstacles are faced in this CLP can be overcome by finding concrete solutions. Thus, gaps found in the implemented project to be attended to.

16. Go for Replication in Other Mandals/Blocks

After successful implementation of CLP project in one mandal/block, it can be replicated in other places where child labour incidence is high.

Precautions: There are two main points which have to be kept in mind while undertaking this project:

(a) To maintain continuity of the project.
(b) People doing this project to be kept highly motivated.

CONCLUSION

These are broad guidelines. However, they can be modified, altered to suit the local scenario. Some were collected, some formed and some modified, but all are tested in the field.

Annexure 1.1
MANDALS AT A GLANCE

	Peddavaduguru	Hindupur
Area of the Mandal	310 sq km	196 sq km
No. of Revenue villages	24	16
No. of Gram Panchayats	25	16
No. of Habitations	39	60

Population (1991 Census)

		Peddavaduguru	Hindupur
	Male	21,364	37,290
	Female	19,455	32,302
	Total	40,819	69,592
Density of Population per sq km		131	370

Literacy Rate of Mandal

		Peddavaduguru	Hindupur
	Male	53.60%	60%
	Female	31.70%	43%
	Total	43.20%	51.50%

Dropout Details

S. No.	Name of the Mandal	Class I (1993–94)			Class IV (1996–97)			Droupout Rate (%)		
		Boys	Girls	Total	Boys	Girls	Total	Boys	Girls	Total
For All										
1.	Peddavaduguru	824	659	1,483	405	265	670	50.85	59.79	54.82
2.	Hindupur	1,967	2,069	4,036	1,359	1,440	2,799	30.59	30.40	30.65
For SCs										
1.	Peddavaduguru	215	121	336	73	30	103	66.05	75.21	69.35
2.	Hindupur	349	336	685	178	153	331	49.00	54.56	51.68
For STs										
1.	Peddavaduguru	8	8	16	1	1	2	87.50	87.50	87.50
2.	Hindupur	22	55	77	9	16	25	59.09	70.91	67.53

Source: Data collected from DPEP, Anantapur.

Annexure 2.1
SURVEY FORM
Form 1 (For one family)

1. Village : .... Mandal : .... District : ....

Household Survey: Village Education Register

House Name	:
Family No	:
Date of Survey	:

2. Group : DWCRA/CMEY/Others
3. Head of the Family : ....
4. Caste : SC / ST / BC / Others
5. Members of Family : Male .... Female ....
6. Family is residing in the village (Yes/No) (If not in which months family is out)
7. Details of Children 3–14 Age:

Follow up-Programme (Year wise)

I II III IV V

S.No.	Child's Name	Sex	Age/ Date of Birth	Parent's Name	In Which Class Studying. AW/NFE	Reasons for Not Studying	Category: Blind/ Deaf & Dumb/ Orthopedically Handicapped	Classwise Progress										Special Remarks and Result
								I	II	III	IV	V	VI	VII	VIII	IX	X	
1	2	3	4	5	6	7	8	9	10	11	12	13	14	15	16	17	18	19

Total

8. Reasons for not studying (in column 7)

1. Working in fields
2. Contract labour (bonded)
3. Housework
4. Looking after small children
5. Cattle grazing
6. Poverty
7. Absence of school or school at a distance
8. Parents not interested
9. Child not interested in school, or fear of school
10. Health problems–physically handicapped
11. Any other reasons

This form can be used for monitoring up to next 5 years

△ = Boy not attending school   ○ = Girl not attending school
▲ = Boy attending school   ● = Girl attending school
□ = Child not attending anganwadi   ■ = Child going to anganwadi

Annexure 2.2
SURVEY FORM
Form 2 (Consolidation of 10 families)
Details of Village Survey

1. Village : ....
2. Mandal : ....
3. District : ....

Family Number	Head of the Family	Caste of Family	No. of Family Members			3–14 years Children Total			3–5 Age-group Anganwadi Children						5–14 Age-group									Reasons for Not Going to School	Physically Handicapped Children			Category Blind/Deaf & Dumb/Ortho-pedically Handicapped
									Going			Not Going			Primary Classes			Higher Classes			Not Going						
			M	F	T	M	F	T	M	F	T	M	F	T	M	F	T	M	F	T	M	F	T		M	F	T	
1	2	3	4	5	6	7	8	9	10	11	12	13	14	15	16	17	18	19	20	21	22	23	24	25	26	27	28	29
1																												

Total

Note: Details of 10 forms of the first kind (Form 1) can be consolidated into this Form 2.

Consolidated Data for Dropout/Never Enrolled Child Labour

Note: Annexures 3.1, 3.2 and 3.3 consist of simple Register. The top sheet can be Annexure 3.1, 5 pages of Mandal abstract can be Annexure 3.2 and 80 pages of details of children can be Annexure 3.3.

Annexure 3.2
MANDAL ABSTRACT

S. No.	Name of the Village	Dropouts			Never Enrolled			Total			Enrolment in Bridge Course/ Resi. Centre	Yet to be Enrolled
		B	G	T	B	G	T	B	G	T		

| Total | | | | | | | | | | | | |

Annexure 3.3

DROPOUT/NEVER-ENROLLED CHILDREN DETAILS

District: Mandal: Village Name: Date of Survey :

S.No.	Name of the Child	Parent Name and (Group Name)	Sex	Age	Caste	Dropout Class	Dropout Year	Never Enrolled	Self-help Groups/ DWCRA/ Others	Present Work	Action Taken

Total

Village Abstract

Dropouts			Never Enrolled			Total		
Boys	Girls	Total	Boys	Girls	Total	Boys	Girls	Total

Annexure 5.1

'DOOR-TO-DOOR' SURVEY CONSOLIDATION FORM (BLANK)

S. No.	Village Name	Total Family Number	Total Population	Male	Female	Education Status of 3–14 Years Children																	
						Anganwadi						Primary School						Going to High School		
						Going			Not Going			Going			Not Going					
						B	G	T	B	G	T	B	G	T	B	G	T	B	G	T
1																				
2																				
3																				
4																				
5																				
6																				
7																				
8																				
9																				
10																				
11																				
12																				
13																				
14																				
15																				
16																				
17																				
18																				
19																				
20																				
Total																				

B–Boys; G–Girls; T–Total

'DOOR-TO-DOOR' SURVEY FIGURES OF PEDDAVADUGURU MANDAL (ATP)

Education Status of 3–14 Years Children

S. No.	Village Name	Total Family Number	Total Population	Male	Female	Anganwadi Going B	Anganwadi Going G	Anganwadi Going T	Anganwadi Not Going B	Anganwadi Not Going G	Anganwadi Not Going T	Primary School Going B	Primary School Going G	Primary School Going T	Primary School Not Going B	Primary School Not Going G	Primary School Not Going T	Going to High School B	Going to High School G	Going to High School T
1	Kottalapalli	156	813	404	409	8	20	28	2	1	3	52	72	124	8	6	14	32	38	70
2	Appecherla	318	1,697	878	819	0	0	0	19	22	41	111	90	201	69	72	141	40	28	68
3	Kandlaguduru	223	1,074	559	515	10	12	22	14	10	24	107	76	183	57	54	111	32	16	48
4	G. Venkatampalli	252	993	532	461	44	31	75	1	1	2	79	62	141	2	1	3	33	22	55
5	Mallenipalli	153	826	428	398	25	19	44	0	2	2	57	39	96	24	25	49	22	16	38
6	Veerapalli	34	199	102	97	0	0	0	3	3	6	18	16	34	2	8	10	10	2	12
7	Ramapuram	116	455	251	204	13	7	20	2	3	5	44	39	83	2	4	6	13	6	19
8	Konapuram	88	473	249	224	12	10	22	4	2	6	97	43	140	17	13	30	14	3	17
9	G. Anantapur	342	1,310	705	605	33	25	58	0	0	0	164	91	255	10	6	16	50	32	82
10	Virupapuram	206	1,039	543	496	34	22	56	5	4	9	90	89	179	23	20	43	33	8	41
11	Dimmagudi	409	1,703	902	801	0	0	0	20	28	48	158	141	299	15	48	63	52	21	73
12	Chituru	227	999	515	484	0	0	0	0	0	0	78	51	129	12	23	35	17	7	24
13	Kristapadu	200	929	494	435	0	0	0	28	24	52	95	51	146	25	48	73	27	6	33
14	Kondupalli	95	452	233	219	15	14	29	0	0	0	29	33	62	2	12	14	14	11	25
15	Chinnavaduguru	286	1,337	701	636	20	24	44	10	5	15	127	81	208	17	55	72	0	0	0
16	Kasepalli	254	1,441	780	661	0	0	0	0	0	0	104	86	190	9	15	24	36	20	56
17	C. Ramarajapalli	105	533	280	253	17	11	28	1	3	4	51	27	78	8	13	21	6	5	11
18	Bhimunipalli	223	1,346	770	526	0	0	0	0	0	0	130	115	245	53	61	114	24	5	29
19	Muppalagooty	169	848	433	415	22	18	40	1	0	1	97	84	181	12	19	31	22	6	28
20	Miduthuru					29	11	40	0	0	0	149	110	259	16	17	33	12	4	16
	Total	3,856	18,467	9,759	8,658	282	224	506	110	108	218	1,837	1,396	3,233	383	520	903	489	256	745

Note: Total 903 child labourers found in 20 villages of Peddavaduguru mandal.

B—Boys; G—Girls; T—Total

Annexure 5.1

'DOOR-TO-DOOR' SURVEY CONSOLIDATION FORM (BLANK)

S. No.	Village Name	Total Family Number	Total Population	Male	Female	Education Status of 3–14 Years Children												
						Anganwadi						Primary School						Going to High School		
						Going			Not Going			Going			Not Going					
						B	G	T	B	G	T	B	G	T	B	G	T	B	G	T
1																				
2																				
3																				
4																				
5																				
6																				
7																				
8																				
9																				
10																				
11																				
12																				
13																				
14																				
15																				
16																				
17																				
18																				
19																				
20																				
Total																				

B–Boys; G–Girls; T–Total

Annexure 5.2

'DOOR-TO-DOOR' SURVEY FIGURES OF PEDDAVADUGURU MANDAL (ATP)

S. No.	Village Name	Total Family Number	Total Population	Male	Female	Anganwadi Going			Anganwadi Not Going			Primary School Going			Primary School Not Going			Going to High School		
						B	G	T	B	G	T	B	G	T	B	G	T	B	G	T
1	Kottalapalli	156	813	404	409	8	20	28	2	1	3	52	72	124	8	6	14	32	38	70
2	Appecherla	318	1,697	878	819	0	0	0	19	22	41	111	90	201	69	72	141	40	28	68
3	Kandlaguduru	223	1,074	559	515	10	12	22	14	10	24	107	76	183	57	54	111	32	16	48
4	G. Venkatampalli	252	993	532	461	44	31	75	1	1	2	79	62	141	2	1	3	33	22	55
5	Mallenipalli	153	826	428	398	25	19	44	0	2	2	57	39	96	24	25	49	22	16	38
6	Veerapalli	34	199	102	97	0	0	0	3	3	6	18	16	34	2	8	10	10	2	12
7	Ramapuram	116	455	251	204	13	7	20	2	3	5	44	39	83	2	4	6	13	6	19
8	Konapuram	88	473	249	224	12	10	22	4	2	6	97	43	140	17	13	30	14	3	17
9	G. Anantapur	342	1,310	705	605	33	25	58	5	4	9	164	91	255	23	20	43	50	32	82
10	Virupapuram	206	1,039	543	496	34	22	56	0	0	0	90	89	179	10	6	16	33	8	41
11	Dimmagudi	409	1,703	902	801	0	0	0	20	28	48	158	141	299	15	48	63	52	21	73
12	Chituru	227	999	515	484	0	0	0	0	0	0	78	51	129	12	23	35	17	7	24
13	Kristapadu	200	929	494	435	0	0	0	28	24	52	95	51	146	25	48	73	27	6	33
14	Kondupalli	95	452	233	219	15	14	29	0	0	0	29	33	62	2	12	14	14	11	25
15	Chinnavaduguru	286	1,337	701	636	20	24	44	10	5	15	127	81	208	17	55	72	0	0	0
16	Kasepalli	254	1,441	780	661	0	0	0	0	0	0	104	86	190	9	15	24	36	20	56
17	C. Ramarajapalli	105	533	280	253	17	11	28	1	3	4	51	27	78	8	13	21	6	5	11
18	Bhimunipalli	223	1,346	770	526	0	0	0	0	0	0	130	115	245	53	61	114	24	5	29
19	Muppalagooty	169	848	433	415	22	18	40	1	0	1	97	84	181	12	19	31	22	6	28
20	Miduthuru					29	11	40	0	0	0	149	110	259	16	17	33	12	4	16
	Total	3,856	18,467	9,759	8,658	282	224	506	110	108	218	1,837	1,396	3,233	383	520	903	489	256	745

Note: Total 903 child labourers found in 20 villages of Peddavaduguru mandal.

B—Boys; G—Girls; T—Total

Annexure 7.2

SUMMARY OF THE CHILDREN

Village: Mandal: District:

S.No.	Name of the Child	Father/ Mother/ Guardian's Name	Sex (M/F)	Caste (SC/ST BC/OC)	Age	Date of Admission & Admn.No.	Group SHG's/ DWCRA/ Other	Never Enrolled	Dropout Class & Year	Category Joined Regular School	Bridge Course	Progress Year-wise I Class	II Class	III Class	IV Class	V Class	VI Class	VII Class	Result
1	2	3	4	5	6	7	8	9	10	11	12	13	14	15	16	17	18	19	20

Annexure 7.3
CASE HISTORY
Monitoring Register (Front Page)

No. :

Admn. No:

Date:

1. Name of the Child:
2. Age:
3. Father/Mother's Name:
4. Occupation:
5. Caste:
6. Sex (Male/Female):
7. Group UNDP/DWCRA/SELF-HELP GROUPS/OTHERS

8. Never Enrolled [＿＿] Dropout [＿＿] Class [＿＿] Year [＿＿]

Detailed Case History

7
6
5
4
3
2
1
0

Month /
Year

REASONS FOR NOT STUDYING
Colour in the Relevant Box

NO ACCESSIBILITY	NEGLIGENCE	POVERTY	CATTLE GRAZING	AGRICULTURAL WORKS

SIBLING	CONTRACT COOLIE	HANDICAPPED	HOUSEWORK	SCHOOL FEAR

Annexure 7.4
PROGRESS REPORT

Bridge Course ☐   Admn. No. :
Regular School ☐   CLASS 1   Date   :

Month & Year	Telugu/...	Mathematics	Science	Social	Remarks

Passed Class 1 in the month / year ....   Signature of the Teacher

Bridge Course ☐   Admn. No. :
Regular School ☐   CLASS 2   Date   :

Month & Year	Telugu/...	Mathematics	Science	Social	Remarks

Passed Class 2 in the month / year ....   Signature of the Teacher

Bridge Course ☐   Admn. No. :
Regular School ☐   CLASS 3   Date   :

Month & Year	Telugu/...	Mathematics	Science	Social	Remarks

Passed Class 3 in the month / year ....   Signature of the Teacher

Bridge Course ☐   Admn. No. :
Regular School ☐   CLASS 4   Date   :

Month & Year	Telugu/...	Mathematics	Science	Social	Remarks

Passed Class 4 in the month / year ....   Signature of the Teacher

Bridge Course ☐   Admn. No. :
Regular School ☐   CLASS 5   Date   :

Month & Year	Telugu/...	Mathematics	Science	Social	Remarks

Passed Class 5 in the month / year ....   Signature of the Teacher

Bridge Course ☐   Admn. No. :
Regular School ☐   CLASS 6   Date   :

Month & Year	Telugu/...	Mathematics	Science	Social	Remarks

Passed Class 6 in the month / year ....   Signature of the Teacher

Bridge Course ☐   Admn. No. :
Regular School ☐   CLASS 7   Date   :

Month & Year	Telugu/...	Mathematics	Science	Social	Remarks

Passed Class 7 in the month / year ....   Signature of the Teacher

Annexure 8.1

Community Register

Consolidated Data for Dropout/ Never-Enrolled Child Labour

(Below Poverty Line Groups)

Note: This has to be maintained by either community volunteer or bridge course teacher residing in the village. Top sheet of register can be Annexure 8. Mandal abstract 5 pages can be Annexure 8.1 and 80 pages of children's details can be Annexure 8.2.

Annexure 8.2
MANDAL ABSTRACT

S.No.	Name of the Village	No. of SHGs	Dropouts			Never Enrolled			Total			Enrolment in Bridge Course/ Resi. Centre	Yet to be Enrolled
			B	G	T	B	G	T	B	G	T		

| Total | | | | | | | | | | | | | |

Annexure 8.3

DROPOUT/NEVER-ENROLLED CHILDREN DETAILS

District: Mandal: Village Name: Date of Survey:

No. of SHGs

S.No.	Name of the Child	Mother's Name (Group Name) & SHG Name	Sex	Age	Caste	Dropout Class	Dropout Year	Never Enrolled	Selfhelp Groups/DWCRA/Others	Present Work	Action Taken

Total

Village Abstract

	Dropouts			Never Enrolled			Total		
	Boys	Girls	Total	Boys	Girls	Total	Boys	Girls	Total

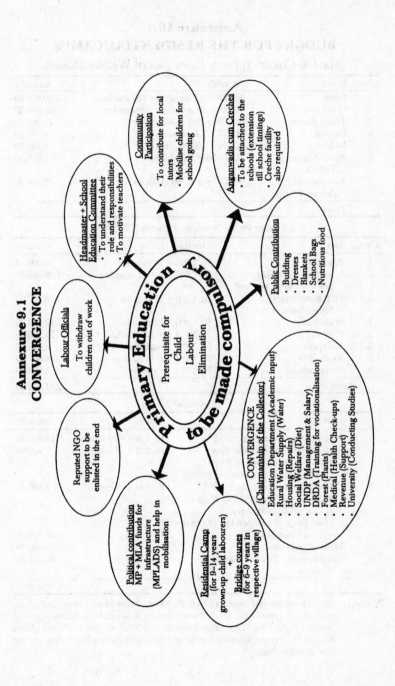

Annexure 9.1
CONVERGENCE

Primary Education to be made compulsory

Prerequisite for Child Labour Elimination

Headmaster + School Education Committee
· To understand their role and responsibilities
· To motivate teachers

Community Participation
· To contribute for local tutors
· Mobilise children for school going

Anganwadis cum Creches
· To be attached to the schools (extension till school timings)
· Creche facility also required

Labour Officials
To withdraw children out of work

Public Contribution
· Building
· Dresses
· Blankets
· School Bags
· Nutritious food

Reputed NGO support to be enlisted in the end

Political contribution MP + MLA funds for infrastructure (MPLADS) and help in mobilisation

Residential Camp (for 9–14 years grown-up child labourers)
+
Bridge courses (for 6–9 years in respective village)

CONVERGENCE (Chairmanship of the Collector)
· Education Department (Academic input)
· Rural Water Supply (Water)
· Housing (Repairs)
· Social Welfare (Diet)
· UNDP (Management & Salary)
· DRDA (Training for vocationalisation)
· Forest (Plants)
· Medical (Health Check-ups)
· Revenue (Support)
· University (Conducting Studies)

Annexure 10.1

BUDGET FOR THE RESIDENTIAL CAMPS

(For 100 Children) From Govt. (Social Welfare Hostel)

S.No.	Item	Monthly	Annually
1.	Food	Rs 270 × 10 months × 100 children	2,70,000.00
2.	Cosmetics	Rs 25 × 10 months × 100 children	25,000.00
3.	Trunk Boxes	Rs 170 × 100 children	17,000.00
4.	Carpets	Rs 67 × 100 children	6,700.00
5.	Bedsheets	Rs 50 × 100 children	5,000.00
6.	Plates, Glasses & Tiffin Boxes	Rs 79.50 × 100 children	7,950.00
7.	Two Pairs of Dresses @250/-	Rs 250 × 2 × 100 children	50,000.00
	Total		3,81,650.00

Salaries for the Residential Camps (UNDP)

S.No.	Item	Monthly	Annually
1.	Principal	Rs 2,500 × 12 months	30,000.00
2.	6 teachers (including one vocational teacher)	Rs 1,500 × 6 × 12 months	1,08,000.00
3.	PET Instructres/ Music Teacher	Rs 1,500 × 12 months	18,000.00
4.	Watchman	Rs 1,000 × 12 months	12,000.00
5.	Cooks—3	Rs 700 × 3 × 12 months	25,200.00
6.	Sweeper	Rs 700 × 12 months	8,400.00
7.	Ayah—2	Rs 700 × 2 × 12 months	16,800.00
8.	Miscellaneous	Rs 250 × 12 months	3,000.00
	Total		2,21,400.00

Desirable

S.No.	Item	Monthly	Annually
1.	Ragi Malt & Greengram Salad	Rs 1,500 × 12 months	18,000.00
2.	Scabama or Medicare (for Lice Removal One Bottle @ Rs 20 for 10 children one bottle required)	Rs 200 × 12 months	2,400.00
3.	Oil Massage & Sunni Pindi @ Rs 75 per litre, coconut @ Rs 25 per kg sunnipindi required (Two litres oil and two kgs of sunnipindi)	Rs 200 × 12 monts	2,400.00
4.	Vocational material		60,000.00
5.	Medical (medicines etc.)		60,000.00
6.	Miscellaneous, Teacher learning material		45,000.00
	Total		1,87,800.00

Notes: Diet to be enhanced from Rs 270 to Rs 500 so that children can get fruits daily with green vegetables at lunch/dinner time. Non-veg to be given weekly.

Diet to be given for 12 months otherwise if children are given a break of two months, their parents/contractors force them to go for work and they are not able to return back.

Annexure 11.1

EDUCATIONAL PROGRESS EVALUATION SHEET

Class ☐　Class Teacher ☐　Quarter | I | II | III | IV |　Date of Evaluation ☐

Note: B.A = Below Average (Below 35%)/A = Average (35% to 50%)/A.A = Above Average (Above 50%) (Marks to be entered)

S. No	Name of the Pupil	Date of Entry into this Class	Telugu					Subject			English			Maths			Science			Social			Teacher's Performance Special Remarks
			Reading			Writing																	
			B.A	A	A.A	B.A	A	A.A	B.A	A	A.A	B.A	A	A.A	B.A	A	A.A	B.A	A	A.A	B.A	A	A.A	
1																							
2																							
3																							
4																							
5																							
6																							
7																							
8																							
9																							
10																							
11																							
12																							
13																							
14																							
15																							
16																							
17																							
18																							
19																							
20																							
21																							
22																							
	Total																						

Syllabus covered:

MRPs/Teachers' remarks:

Annexure 12.1

Monitoring Register for
Child Labour Education Centre

Note: Annexure 12.1 can be the top sheet of the register, 10 pages of summary can be Annexure 12.2 and 100 pages of case history can be Annexure 12.3 in front and Annexure 12.4 at the back, which makes one monitoring register.

Annexure 12.2
SUMMARY OF THE CHILDREN

Village: Mandal: Dist:

S.No	Name of the Child	Father/ Mother/ Guardian's Name	Sex (M/F)	Caste (SC/ST/ BC/ OC)	Age	Date of Admission & Admn.No.	Group SHGs/ DWCRA/ Other	Never Enrolled	Dropout Class & Year	Category Joined		Progress Year-wise							Result
										Regular School	Bridge Course	I Class	II Class	III Class	IV Class	V Class	VI Class	VII Class	
1	2	3	4	5	6	7	8	9	10	11	12	13	14	15	16	17	18	19	20

Annexure 12.3
Monitoring Sheet
CASE HISTORY

No. :

Admn. No:
Date:

1. Name of the Child: 2. Age:
3. Father/Mother's Name: 4. Occupation:
5. Caste: 6. Sex (Male/Female):
7. Group UNDP/DWCRA/SELF-HELP GROUPS/OTHERS
8. Never Enrolled [ ] Dropout [ ] Class [ ] Year [ ]

Detailed Case History

Month / Year

0 1 2 3 4 5 6 7

REASONS FOR NOT STUDYING
Colour in the Relevant Box

[ ]

NO ACCESSIBILITY	NEGLIGENCE	POVERTY	CATTLE GRAZING	AGRICULTURAL WORKS
SIBLING	CONTRACT COOLIE	HANDICAPPED	HOUSEWORK	SCHOOL FEAR

Annexure 12.4
PROGRESS REPORT

Bridge Course ☐   Admn. No. :
Regular School ☐   CLASS 1   Date   :

Month & Year	Telugu/...	Mathematics	Science	Social	Remarks

Passed Class 1 in the month / year ....   Signature of the Teacher

Bridge Course ☐   Admn. No. :
Regular School ☐   CLASS 2   Date   :

Month & Year	Telugu/...	Mathematics	Science	Social	Remarks

Passed Class 2 in the month / year ....   Signature of the Teacher

Bridge Course ☐   Admn. No. :
Regular School ☐   CLASS 3   Date   :

Month & Year	Telugu/...	Mathematics	Science	Social	Remarks

Passed Class 3 in the month / year ....   Signature of the Teacher

Bridge Course ☐   Admn. No. :
Regular School ☐   CLASS 4   Date   :

Month & Year	Telugu/...	Mathematics	Science	Social	Remarks

Passed Class 4 in the month / year ....   Signature of the Teacher

Bridge Course ☐   Admn. No. :
Regular School ☐   CLASS 5   Date   :

Month & Year	Telugu/...	Mathematics	Science	Social	Remarks

Passed Class 5 in the month / year ....   Signature of the Teacher

Bridge Course ☐   Admn. No. :
Regular School ☐   CLASS 6   Date   :

Month & Year	Telugu/...	Mathematics	Science	Social	Remarks

Passed Class 6 in the month / year ....   Signature of the Teacher

Bridge Course ☐   Admn. No. :
Regular School ☐   CLASS 7   Date   :

Month & Year	Telugu/...	Mathematics	Science	Social	Remarks

Passed Class 7 in the month / year ....   Signature of the Teacher

Annexure 13.1
RESIDENTIAL CAMPS
(Overall Development)

Requirement for Progressive Child Labour Cams
(All Round Development)

Nutrition
Supplementing food proteins
1. Ragi Malt
2. Green Gram Salad

Hygiene
1. Oil Massage
2. Ubtan
3. Lice Removal (Medicare etc.)

Vocational
Training for vocationalisation
For e.g., tailoring, embroidery, etc.

Sports & Physical Training
1. Skipping Rope
2. Rings
3. Hand Balls
4. Physical Training

Cultural
1. Dances
2. Songs

Education
Intensive coaching and efforts to see all children pass one class in four months till Class 3.

Joyful Method of Learning
To Learn Educative Stories by Puppet Shows

Annexure 14.1
LABOUR LAWS AND CONSTITUTIONAL
ARTICLES FOR CHILD LABOUR
(A Brief of Labour Laws)

Children (Pledging of Labour) Act, 1933 may be said to be the first statutory enactment dealing with child labour. This law prohibits parents and guardians from pledging the service of a child.

The Children (Pledging of Labour) Act, 1933 was followed in quick succession by the Employment of Child Act, 1938. This law, has now been replaced by the Child Labour (Prohibition and Regulation) Act, 1986.

The Employment of Child Act, 1938, suffered from the following infirmities:

- The Act did not attempt a formal definition of the child.
- It was unclear and ambiguous in its scope and content inasmuch as it classified children into two categories for the purpose of prohibition and regulation of their employment. The first category of children were those below the age of 14 who were prohibited from working in five occupations listed in the Act. The second category were those who had completed 14 years but were below 17. They could be employed in the prohibited occupations provided they were allowed a period of rest.

The Child Labour (Prohibition and Regulation) Act, 1986

There are a number of Acts which prohibit employment of children below 14 years and 15 years in certain specified employments. However, there is no procedure laid down in any law for deciding in which employments, occupations or processes the employment of children should be banned. There is also no law to regulate the working conditions of children in most of the employments where they are not prohibited from working and are working under exploitative conditions.

The Child Labour (Prohibition and Regulation) Act, 1986 seeks to prohibit employment of children below the age of 14 years in 7 occupations and 18 processes listed in the Schedule of the Act, and regulate the working conditions of children in other employments. Through a Notification dated 26 May 1993, the working conditions of children have been regulated in all employments which are not prohibited under the Child Labour (Prohibition and Regulation) Act, 1986.

The Supreme Court of India has also expressed its concern about this age old evil. In its judgement dated 10 December 1996 in Writ Petition (Civil) No. 465/ 1986, the Court had given certain directions regarding the manner in which the working conditions of children in non-hazardous occupations are to be regulated and improved upon. The important directions given in the judgement are:

1. Survey for identification of working children;
2. Withdrawal of children working in hazardous industries and ensuring their education in appropriate institutions;
3. Contribution @ Rs 20,000 per child to be paid by the offending employers of children to a welfare fund which is to be established for this purpose;
4. Employment to one adult member of the family of the child so withdrawn from work and if that is not possible, a contribution of Rs 5,000 to the welfare fund to be made by the state government;
5. Financial assistance to the families of the children so withdrawn to be paid out of the interest earnings on the corpus of Rs 20,000/25,000 deposited in the welfare fund as long as the child is actually sent to school;
6. Regulating working hours for children working in non-hazardous occupations so that their working hours do not exceed six hours per day and education for at least two hours is ensured. The entire expenditure on education is to be borne by the concerned employer.

While Child Labour (Prohibition and Regulation) Act, 1986 continues to be the principal enactment on the issue of prohibition and regulation of employment of children, there are a number of other labour laws that are not so much concerned about withdrawing children from work as with merely specifying the minimum age of entry to employment in certain factories, mines, plantations, etc. It is worth examining and analysing these provisions.

Factories Act, 1948—Section 67
Prohibits employment of young children. 'No child who has not completed his fourteenth year shall be required or allowed to work in any factory.'

Plantation Labour Act, 1951—Section 24
Prohibition of employment of young children. 'No child who has not completed his 12th year shall be required or allowed to work in any plantation.'

Section 26—Non-adult workers who carry tokens
No child who has not completed his 12th year and no adolescent shall be required or allowed to work in any plantation unless

1. a certificate of fitness granted with reference to him under Section 27 is in the custody of the employer; and
2. such child or adolescent carried with him while he is at work a token giving a reference to such certificate.

Merchant Shipping Act, 1951—Section 109
No person under 15 years of age shall be engaged or carried to sea to work in any capacity in any ship, except

1. in a school ship or a training ship in accordance with the prescribed conditions; or
2. in a ship in which all persons employed are members of one family; or
3. in a home trade ship of less than 200 tons gross; or
4. where such person is to be employed on nominal wages and will be in charge of his father or other adult near male relative.

Mines Act, 1952—Section 45

1. No child shall be employed in any mine, nor shall any child be allowed to be present in any part of a mine which is below ground or in any open cast working in which any mining operation is being carried on.
2. After such date as the central government, may by notification in the official gazette, appoint in this behalf, no child shall be allowed to be present in any part of a mine above ground where any operation connected with or incidental to any mining operation is being carried on.

Motor Transport Workers Act, 1961—Section 21

No child shall be required or allowed to work in any capacity in any motor transport undertaking.

Apprentices Act, 1961—Section 3
Qualifications for being engaged as an apprentice

A person shall not be qualified for being engaged as an apprentice to undergo apprenticeship training in any designated trade, unless he:

1. is not less than 14 years of age.
2. satisfies such standards of education and physical fitness as may be prescribed; provided that different standards may be prescribed in relation to apprenticeship training in different designated trades and for different categories of apprentices.

Beedi & Cigar Workers (Conditions of Employment) Act, 1966

Prohibition of employment of children—no child shall be required or allowed to work in any industrial premises.

The Minimum Wages Act

The Minimum Wages Act was enacted in 1948 with the objective of fixing, reviewing, revising and enforcing the minimum rates of wages relating to scheduled employments to be notified under the law by the appropriate Government, i.e., central/state. The intention of the Act is to fix minimum rates of wages in employments in which the labour force is vulnerable to exploitation, i.e., is not well organised and has no effective bargaining power. It provides for an institutional mechanism and procedure for fixation, review, revision and enforcement of minimum rates of wages. 'Minimum wage' has not been defined in this Act.

Above all, laws have no uniform age of entry and there is no strict enforcement.

Contract Labour Act, 1970

With a view to remove the difficulties of contract labour and bearing in mind the recommendations of various commissions and committees and the decisions of Supreme Court, particularly in the case of Standard Vacuum Refining Company in 1960, the Contract Labour (Regulation and Abolition) Act, was enacted in 1970. This Act seeks to regulate the employment of contract labour in certain establishments and to provide for its abolition under certain circumstances. The Act applies to every establishment in which 20 or more workmen are employed or were employed on any day of the preceding 12 months as contract labour and to every contractor who employs or who employed on any day of the preceding 12 months 20 or more workmen. It does not apply to establishments where the work performed is of intermittent or causal nature. The Act also applies to establishments of the Government and local authorities as well.

The Act makes provision for the appointment of inspecting staff for maintenance of registers and records for penalties for the contravention of the provisions of the Act and rules made thereunder and for making rules for carrying out the purpose of the Act. In the central sphere, officers of the CIRM have been appointed as inspectors.

Apart from the regulatory measures provided under the Act for the benefit of the contract labour, the 'appropriate government' is authorised to prohibit employment of contract labour in any establishement in any process, operation or other work.

Bonded Labour Act, 1976

The Bonded Labour System was abolished throughout the country with effect from 25 October 1975, under the Bonded Labour System (Ordinance) 1975, which was later converted to the Bonded Labour System (Abolition) Act, 1976. It freed unilaterally all the bonded labourers from bondage with simultaneous liquidation of their debts. This Act is being administered by the state governments.

Forcing a person to work under bondage is punishable with imprisonment for a term, and a fine which may extend to Rs 2,000.

A freed bonded labourer is provided rehabilitation grant to the extent of Rs 10,000 which is contributed both by the central and the state government concerned on a 50:50 basis.

ARTICLES

Article 23—Prohibition of traffic in human beings and forced labour.
Traffic in human beings and beggars and other similar forms of forced labour are prohibited and any contravention of this provision shall be offence punishable in accordance with law.

Article 24—Prohibition of children in factories, etc.
No child below the age of 14 years shall be employed to work in any factory or mine or engaged in any other hazardous employment.

Articles 39(e) and (f)—Certain principles of policy to be followed by state. The state shall, in particular, direct its policy securing (e) that the health and strength of workers, men and women and the tender age of children are not abused and that citizens are not forced by economic necessity to enter avocations unsuited to their age or strength, (f) that children are given opportunities and facilities to develop in a healthy manner and in conditions of freedom and dignity and that childhood and youth are protected against exploitation and against moral and material abandonment.

Article 41—The right to work, to education and to public assistance in particular circumstances.
The state shall within the limits of its economic capacity and development make effective provision for securing the right to work, to education and to public assistance in cases of unemployment, old age, sickness and disablement, and in other cases of undeserved want.

Article 45—Provision for free and compulsory education for children.
The state shall endeavour to provide within a period of 10 years from the commencement of this constitution for free and compulsory education for all children until they complete the age of 14 years.

Article 47—Responsibility of the state to raise the nutritional levels, and standard of living of its citizens and to improve public health.
The state shall regard the raising the level of nutrition and the standard of living of its people and improvement of public health as among its primary duties and in particular the state shall endeavour to bring about prohibition of the consumption (except for medical purposes) of intoxicating drinks and of drugs which are injurious to health.

A brief of labour laws and articles related to child labour are given above for guidance. However, enforcement of above labour laws to be followed in our country strictly.

Annexure 15.1
BUDGET

1. It should focus on three main points:

   (a) Residential camps (9–14 years child labourers).
   (b) Bridge courses (6–9 years child labourers).
   (c) Anganwadi-cum-creche (0–5 years children).

2. Training:

   (a) Survey.
   (b) Induction training for residential/bridge course teachers.
   (c) Monthly refresher course training.
   (d) Training to anganwadi workers.

3. Community mobilisation:

   (a) Teachers meeting.
   (b) Youth group meeting.
   (c) Women group meeting.
   (d) Monitoring team meeting.
   (e) Rallies.
   (f) Film shows on child labour.

4. One child labour officer (CLO) in each district.
5. One Child Labour Programme Manager (CLPM) at the state level.
6. Total budget for one year (programme to run continuously for 12 months) comes to approximately.

   (a) One mandal: Rs 42,22,750.00
      (with two residential camps, 40 bridge courses and extension of timings in 40 anganwadi-cum-creche, including training, community mobilisation and process documentation).
   (b) For example, for Andhra Pradesh it can run in approximately 700 mandals (out of 1,122 mandals) and it has 23 districts, so the cost for one year will be 295 crore.
   (c) State level: Rs 295 + 5 crore
                      = Rs 300 crore

(5 crore for one state-level programme manager staff and establishment, 23 districts child labour officers, state establishment, etc.)

Thus minimum Rs 300 crore are required for one year continuous child labour eradication programme along with the other four factors to be enforced strictly by the government, i.e.,

- Education to be made compulsory.
- No child labour to be allowed (labour officials to strictly enforce laws).
- Vocationalisation to be introduced and material made to be marketed with the help of the official machinery.
- Programme to run for minimum three years continuously so that results can be seen.

This programme is only possible if district convergence is used, unutilised buildings are repaired by the government and the government takes over the maintenance of the buildings.

Annexure 16.1
'CHILD AT WORK'
A STUDY OF CHILD LABOURERS

I. Identification Data

1. Name   :
2. Age   :
3. Religion   :
4. Caste   :
5. Mother Tongue   :
6. Education   :
7. Native Place/Address   :

II. Family Data

1. Is your family   : Joint/Nuclear/Extended
2. Size of the family   : Large/Medium/Small
3. Is your house   : Own/Rented/Inherited
                             (Govt. allotted house)
4. Is your house   : Thatched/Tiled/Terraced
5. Location   :
6. Does it have   : (a) Electricity, (b) Water facility
7. Family particulars   :

Relationship with the Child	Age	Marital Status	Education	Occupation	Annual Income

Annexure 16.2

III. Determination of Child Labour

(i) Demographic Determinants
1. Age　　　　　　　　　　:
2. Birth Order　　　　　　:
3. Marital Status　　　　　:

(ii) Socio Cultural Determinants
1. Specify your family nature　: Broken family/Women-headed/Normal family

2. Give the reasons for being illiterate/School Dropout　: Parents/Reluctance/Lack of scools/Distant location of schools/Household work/Lack of interest/Poverty/Father's death

3. The work you do now is part of your family tradition　: Yes / No

4. Why did you involve in this　: Higher concentration/Proximity/Work in particular/Easy availability/Any other

5. (a) Did you take up this work voluntarily　: Yes / No
   (b) If not, who initiated　: Father/Mother/Brothers/Relatives/Neighbours

6. How many numbers of your peer group are involved in this work　:

(iii) Economic Factors:
1. What is the main reason for taking up this work　: To supplement family income/Unemployment of elder members in the family/Death of the head of the family/For better living/Loan obligation

Annexure 16.3

(iv) Treatment at Home

1. Who is the decision
   maker in your family   :   Father/Mother/Both/
                                     Any other

2. Do you enjoy freedom in the following:
   - (a) To spend money   :   Yes / No
   - (b) To express opinion   :   Yes / No
   - (c) To choose friends   :   Yes / No
   - (d) To go for outing   :   Yes / No
   - (e) Spend your leisure time   :   Yes / No

3. Do you have a 'say'/equal care in the following:
   - (a) In education   :   Yes / No
   - (b) In employment   :   Yes / No
   - (c) In food allocation   :   Yes / No
   - (d) Gifts/Punishments   :   Yes / No
   - (e) Health care   :   Yes / No

(v) Situation at Workplace

1. (a) Specify the nature of your work :
   (b) State if it requires skill   :
   (c) Have you undergone training   :
2. Specify the working hours   :
3. Will you be given any rest
   interval other than lunch break
4. Specify your daily wages/salary   :
5. (a) Do you work overtime

Annexure 16.4

(b) How much will you be paid
for overtime :

6. Do you get a day off in a week :

7. Are you made to work even at
the time of festivals :

8. (a) At what age you joined here :
   (b) For how long have you
   been working :

9. Specify the facilities that
   you lack at the workplace : Spacious rooms/Good
   ventilation/Hygienic/
   toilets/surroundings/
   Drinking water/Sunlight

10. Does your work result in
    health hazards : Headache/Strain to eyes/
    Backache/Frequent illness/
    Any other

11. If you get any ailments are
    you provided medical care
    by the employer : Yes / No

12. What are the benefits you get
    other than salary :

13. (a) Do your employers make
    you do domestic chores
    for them : Yes / No
    (b) If so how often : Daily/Sometimes/
    Occasionally
    (c) Are you paid anything for that :
    (d) What are these domestic chores :

14. Does your employer listen to
    your grievances : Always/Sometimes/Never

Annexure 16.5

15. If you can't do the work
   properly or cause any damage
   to machinery are you   : Yes / No
   punished/ if so how   Verbal abuse/Not giving
                                           salary/Any other

(vi) **Attitudes**

(i) **Towards job**
   1. (a) Are you happy doing
          the present work   : Very much/Somewhat/
                                          Not at all

(ii) **Towards education**
   1. (a) How far education is
          useful   : Very much/Somewhat/
                                          Not at all
      (b) Given opportunity,
          will you attend
          non-formal education   : Yes / No

(iii) **Status perception**
   1. Are you satisfied with
      your present status   : Very much/Somewhat/Not
                                          at all

   2. Do you feel that you are
      exploited at home and
      at the workplace   : Yes / No

   3. To have better status
      what should children have   : Education/Good job/
                                          Money/Equality/Leisure
                                          time/Any other

   4. What do you wish to do to
      improve your status   : Seek redressal/Tolerate/
                                          Rebel

(vii) **Any other Details:**

Anganwadis: In rural areas 3–5 years children attend pre-schools which are called anganwadis.

Mandal Mahila Samakhya: Women groups at 40–60 villages form VO (village organisations) and these VO form MMS at the mandal level.

DWCRA: 14 or more women form a group and accumulate their savings and after some time government extends loan so that they are economic independent.

Country: India as a country is divided into states.

States: States are further divided into districts.

Districts: Districts is further divided into mandal/block.

Mandal/block: Mandal/block is further divided into villages, for example, a mandals/blocks consist of approximately 40–60 villages.

Village: 73 per cent of India (country) resides in villages. These are small habitations starting with 200 families to as big as 500 families.

ABOUT THE AUTHOR

Pramila H. Bhargava, a civil servant, is a member of the Indian Railways Personnel Services. She is currently Deputy Chief Personnel Officer, Northern Railways, New Delhi. She has also served as National Consultant to the UNDP on Primary Education and Child Labour Elimination (1999–2000).

During her career with the Railways, Pramila Bhargava has held a number of increasingly senior positions and has received various awards in recognition of her work in human resource development. She has previously published *A Tribute to Baba: The Ultimate Motivators*.